GEOGRAPHY

KEY CONCEPTS AND BASIC SKILLS

WILLIAM LEFKOWITZ

A Pacemaker® Book   FEARON EDUCATION

A DIVISION OF
DAVID S. LAKE PUBLISHERS
BELMONT, CALIFORNIA

Illustrators: Valerie Felts, Sherry Sheffield
Boulton, Duane Bibby
Cartographers: Sharon Johnson, Jean Ann Carroll

Photo Credits: National Aeronautics and Space Administration (cover); United States Geological Survey (1, 25, 26, 27, 29, 30, 31, 34, 35, 36, 37, 38, 39, 57, 70, 71, 100); THE BETTMAN ARCHIVE (24, 62 top, 80, 81, 82, 106); Hawaii Visitors Bureau (42, 55); Alaska Division of Tourism (43, 48); Florida Department of Commerce, Division of Tourism (49); Brant Ward/San Francisco Chronicle (54, 107); National Archives (56, 104); Florida State Archives (62 bottom, 74 bottom, 86, 87, 105); California Farm Bureau (63, 64, 66 top, 95 bottom); California Department of Water Resources (65 top and bottom); Emma Rivera/Peace Corps (66 bottom); Stephen Feldman/Peace Corps (67); Bill Strassberger/Peace Corps (68); American Iron and Steel Institute (72 top and bottom); Environmental Protection Agency (74 top); Point Reyes Bird Observatory (75); Resource Recycling magazine (77 bottom); Redenius/Peace Corps (84); Paul Conklin/Peace Corps (89); United States Department of Agriculture, Soil Conservation Service (90); Library of Congress (92); Pete Breinig/San Francisco Chronicle (95 top); John Herr (96); Frampton/Peace Corps (97); Watson/Peace Corps (98, 101); Gary Fong/San Francisco Chronicle (102); Susan Ehmer/San Francisco Chronicle (103.)

ISBN 0-8224-3351-6

Printed in the United States of America
1. 9 8 7 6 5 4 3 2 1

CONTENTS

INTRODUCTION

Think about this for a moment:

Earth is the only place in space we know of that has living things on it.

There may be life somewhere else, but so far we haven't found it anywhere but here.

What makes Earth so special? That is the main question this book tries to answer.

Geography: Key Concepts and Basic Skills tells how the Earth provides us with the things we need to live.

The book also tells how Earth moves through space and how our planet is always changing. It tells what causes earthquakes and volcanoes. It tells how mountains are built up and then worn down.

Geography: Key Concepts and Basic Skills is also about people. It tells how we use the things that Earth provides. It tells of the inventions we have made to improve our lives. It tells of some of the problems we face and what some people are doing about those problems.

Yet this book tells only a small part of all there is to know about Earth and its people. We hope you will go on to learn more about things you find most interesting.

Geographers in Wyoming, 1870

1

Think of the hot sun hanging in space like a giant glowing ball. Think of the cool moon moving across the dark night sky. Think of the stars shining from far away. The sun, moon, and stars are all floating through space. And we, here on Earth, are floating along with them.

What is Earth like? To start with, we know that it is almost as round as a ball. But it is not perfectly round.

How big is Earth? Well, let's say you could walk around Earth at its widest point. And let's say you were to walk 20 miles a day. The trip would take you about 3½ years!

Earth is large compared with the moon. But it is small compared with the sun. Here's how you can compare the size of the sun, moon, and Earth. Place a pea next to a basketball. Place a grain of sand next to the pea. Think of the basketball as the sun. Think of the pea as Earth. And think of the grain of sand as the moon.

Geography

Things to Find Out

1. How big Earth is
2. The different forms of land and water
   found on Earth

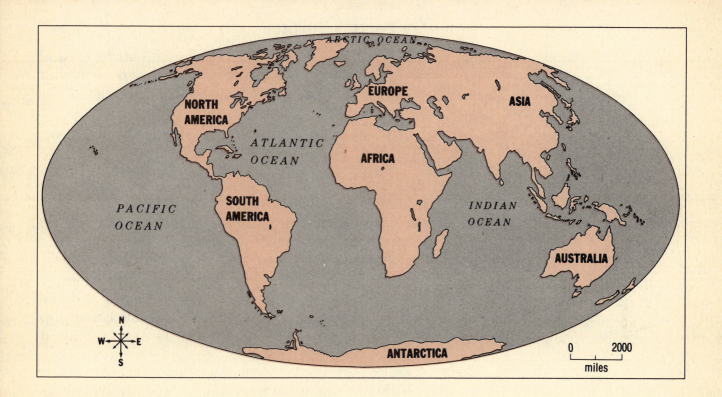

Earth's Oceans and Continents

Long before anyone went up into space, sailors traveled all over Earth. They crossed the oceans and went up and down the coast of every land. They made drawings of what they saw. From these drawings, mapmakers drew maps of Earth. Today, mapmakers can use pictures taken from space when they draw maps. Their maps help us to better understand the world we live in.

Look at the map above. It shows how Earth is divided into ocean and land. Which is there more of, ocean or land?

More than two-thirds of Earth is covered by water. Less than one-third is land.

The land rises up from the water and divides it into four large oceans. Look at the map again. What are the names of the four oceans?

The land areas are called **continents.** A continent is a very large body of land. There are seven continents on Earth. Find their names on the map.

Which continent do you live on?

On Earth's Surface

Earth's surface is shaped into different **landforms** and bodies of water. Look at the landforms and the bodies of water in the drawing on page 5. Then read about them below.

Landforms

Plains are mostly flat lands that often stretch for hundreds of miles. They may also be gently rolling land. They do not rise much above **sea level.** Sea level is where the ocean meets the land.

Plateaus are flat areas that are higher than sea level. They often rise sharply from the lands around them.

Mountains rise very high above sea level and the surrounding land. The sides of mountains are very steep. Sometimes mountains have rounded or pointed tops.

Valleys are low lands that lie between mountains.

Hills are similar to mountains, but they are not as high.

Islands are areas of land surrounded by water.

Peninsulas are areas of land that reach out into the water. A peninsula has water on three sides.

mountains

valley

sea

islands

hills

plains

lake

plateau

river

gulf or bay

river

peninsula

Bodies of Water

The **oceans** are the four largest bodies of salt water on Earth.

Seas are large bodies of salt water that are smaller than oceans. They are partly surrounded by land.

Gulfs and **bays** are bodies of salt water that reach into the land from an ocean or sea. Gulfs are larger than bays.

Lakes are bodies of water surrounded on all sides by land. Most lakes have fresh water. Fresh water can be used for watering crops and for drinking, cooking, and washing.

Rivers are formed by fresh water flowing from one place to another. Rivers flow into other rivers, or into lakes, seas, or oceans.

Summary

1. Earth floats in space as the sun, moon, and stars do.
2. About two-thirds of Earth's surface is covered by water.
3. Earth has seven large land areas called continents.
4. The main types of landforms are plains, plateaus, mountains, valleys, hills, islands, and peninsulas.
5. The main types of bodies of water are oceans, seas, gulfs, bays, lakes, and rivers.

Questions to Discuss

Here are some questions to talk over in class.

1. On what kind of landform is your town located? How does that landform affect these things:
   - How easy or hard it is to get from one place to another
   - How easy or hard it is to build houses and other buildings
   - How easy or hard it is to farm the land
2. What bodies of water are nearby?
   - Do people swim or go boating in any of them?
   - Does your community get drinking water from any of them?
   - Do people travel or ship goods on any of them?
   - How would life be different if they weren't there?

Special Project

Write a report about the landforms and the bodies of water in your area. Tell something about each one. Take photos or draw pictures to show how they look. Add them to your report.

Directions on Earth

Have you ever heard someone say something like this?

"Drive three miles north to Anderson Road. Then go east on Anderson for about a mile."

North and east are directions. Anytime you go from one place to another you move in some direction.

- If you are going toward the North Pole, you are going north.
- If you are going toward the South Pole, you are going south.
- If you are going toward the rising sun, you are going east.
- If you are going toward the setting sun, you are going west.

Look at the map on the right. Let's say you were to fly from New York City to Quito. In which direction would you be flying?

You'd be flying south. In which direction would you be flying on your return trip?

On your return you'd be flying north.

Now let's say you were to fly from New York to San Francisco. In which direction would you be flying?

Did you say west? In which direction would you be flying on your return trip?

That's right. East.

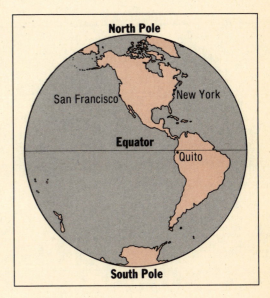

Countries of North America

The North American continent is divided into ten countries. Three are large. Seven are small. The seven smaller countries are known as Central America.

Look at the map. Read the names of the ten countries. Notice that the states of Alaska and Hawaii are separated from the United States **mainland.**

Look at the arrows and letters on the left side of the map. They help you tell direction.

N: north   S: south   E: east   W: west

This kind of marking on a map is called a **compass rose.** Use the compass rose to answer these questions.

1. Which country is just north of the mainland United States?

2. In which direction would you go to get from the United States to Mexico?

3. Which ocean is west of the United States?

4. Which ocean is east of the United States?

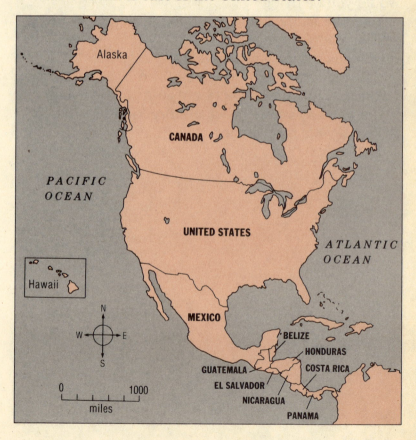

Reading a Physical Map

You have read about Earth's different landforms and bodies of water. The **physical map** below shows where some of these landforms and bodies of water are found in the western United States.

The map key explains the symbols and markings used on the map.

Study the map and the key. Then answer the questions below.

1. Which state has the longest coastline?
2. Which river flows through Colorado, Utah, Nevada, Arizona, and California?
3. Which state has the fewest mountains?
4. What kind of landform lies between the Sierra Nevada mountains and California's coastal mountains?
5. Which does Idaho have more of, mountains or plateaus?

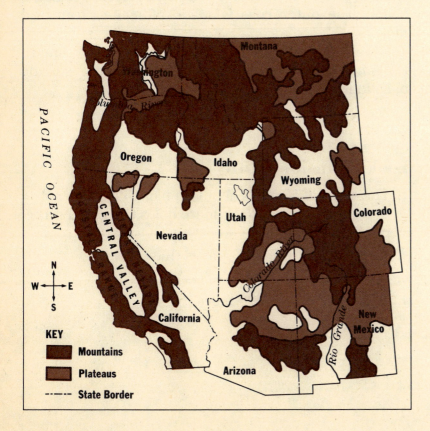

2

Would you like to take a trip to the center of Earth? Your trip would be 4,000 miles long. You would have to dig through solid rock. And you would have to swim through melted rock and metal.

The first part of your trip would be through Earth's crust. The crust is made of solid rock. The continents *and* the floor of the ocean are on the surface of this crust. Below them are many miles of solid rock.

Beyond the crust you would come to the mantle. This layer of Earth is made of very hot rock. Some of this rock is so hot it has melted.

Next you would come to the outer core. Scientists believe the outer core is made of melted iron and nickel.

Finally, at the center of Earth, you would come to the inner core. Scientists think the inner core is made of solid iron and nickel.

Looking Inside Earth

1. The **crust** of Earth is about 5 miles thick under the oceans. It is up to 25 or more miles thick under the continents.

2. Earth's **mantle** is 1,775 miles thick.

3. The **outer core** is 1,400 miles thick.

4. The **inner core** is 800 miles thick.

Things to Find Out

1. What is below Earth's surface
2. What is above Earth's surface
3. What holds things down on Earth

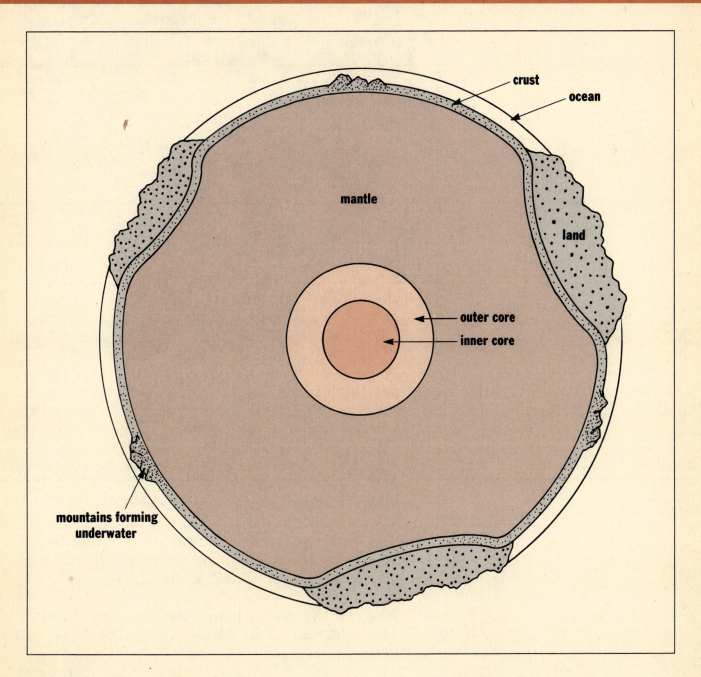

The first layer of the atmosphere stretches for 10 miles above the Earth. It helps keep us and other living things alive.

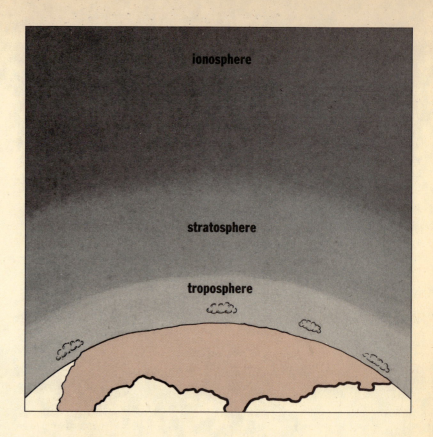

The first layer of the atmosphere stretches for 10 miles above the Earth. It helps keep us and other living things alive.

Above Earth's Surface

Hold up a piece of paper. Blow on the paper. What makes the paper move?

Moving air makes the paper move. You can't see the air. But it is there. Earth is surrounded by layers of air that stretch for hundreds of miles above its surface.

These layers of air are called the **atmosphere.** The atmosphere is the key to life on Earth. It contains gases that living things need. Most of these gases are in the first layer of the atmosphere.

People and animals breathe in **oxygen** from the atmosphere. Without oxygen, we would die in just a few minutes.

Plants take in **carbon dioxide** and other gases.

All living things need the water **vapor** found in the atmosphere. Water vapor is a gas made of tiny drops of water that are too small for us to see. It helps keep out some of the sun's heat. Without it we would all burn up.

When the sun is not shining, the water vapor keeps in heat that has built up during the day. Otherwise we would freeze at night.

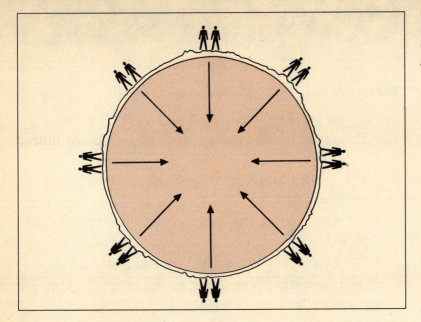

The Atmosphere Has Layers

The atmosphere changes as you move higher above Earth's surface. **Temperatures** range from super cold to super hot. And the air gets thinner and lighter the higher you go.

The atmosphere has three different layers. The most important layer for us is the one closest to Earth—the **troposphere.**

Here's why:

- Most of the gases that living things need are found in the troposphere.
- Water vapor and other matter in the troposphere affect our **weather.**

What Holds Us Down?

Have you ever wondered why we don't fall off Earth's surface? What keeps air and oceans and us from floating into space?

Gravity is what holds us all in place. Gravity is a strong pulling force from inside Earth. The sun and the moon and other bodies in space also have gravity.

Think of how a magnet holds onto things made from iron. Gravity is like that. Earth's gravity pulls everything that is on or near Earth down to its surface.

When you get far away from Earth, and other bodies in space, gravity has less force. That's why things float in space.

Summary

1. Earth is made of both solid and melted parts.
   - The crust is solid rock. It is from 5 to 25 or more miles thick.
   - The mantle is made of very hot solid rock and of melted rock.
   - Scientists think the outer core is melted iron and nickel.
   - They think the inner core is solid iron and nickel.
2. The atmosphere is made of layers of air. The lowest layer is called the troposphere.
   - It contains most of the water vapor and other gases we need.
   - In daytime, it helps keep out some of the sun's heat.
   - At night, it keeps in some of the sun's heat.
3. Gravity is a strong pulling force. It holds us to Earth.

Questions to Discuss

1. The troposphere is filled with dust and other tiny bits of matter. Where do you think these things come from?
2. Imagine that Earth's gravity suddenly had no effect on the people and things in your classroom. What would happen?

Special Projects

1. About 4,000 miles below you is the center of Earth. Draw a picture that shows you at the top and the four layers of Earth below you. Write the name of each layer on your picture.
2. Find out how some smoke from cars and factories is harmful to the atmosphere.
3. Find out how some spray cans can be harmful to the atmosphere.

Locating States and Cities

The map below shows the United States of America. The United States is divided into 50 states. There are 48 states on the mainland. Hawaii is in the Pacific Ocean. Alaska is separated from the mainland by Canada.

The map shows all 50 states, but it names only 9 of them. For a complete map of the United States, turn to the Atlas at the back of the book. This map below shows one city in each of the 9 states. Small dots show where the cities are.

1. Which 9 states are named on the map?
2. In which state is each of these cities?
   a. Anchorage b. San Francisco c. Fargo d. Miami
3. In which direction would you go to get from:
   a. Cleveland, Ohio, to Miami, Florida?
   b. Miami, Florida, to Houston, Texas?
   c. Houston, Texas, to Fargo, North Dakota?
   d. Fargo, North Dakota, to Cleveland, Ohio?

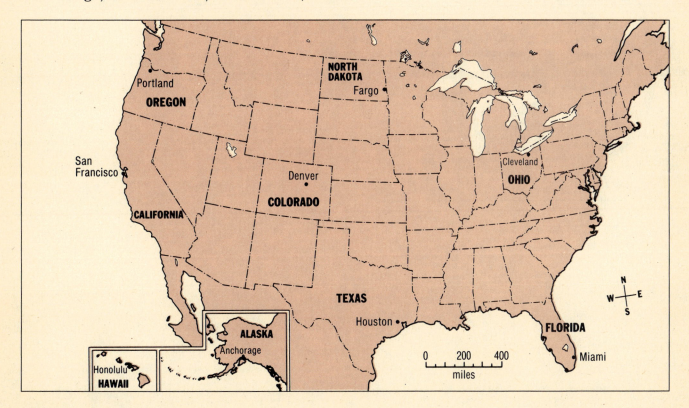

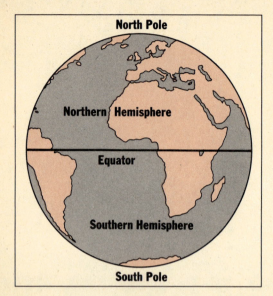

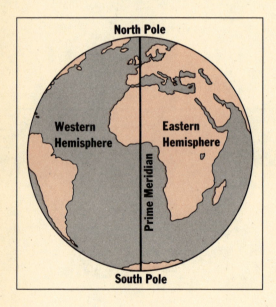

Dividing Earth into Hemispheres

It's often easier to study something large if we divide it into smaller parts.

When we study Earth, we can divide it in half if we imagine a line that circles the planet halfway between the North and South Poles. This line is called the **equator.**

Everything above the equator is in the Northern **Hemisphere.** Everything below the equator is in the Southern Hemisphere. A hemisphere is half of anything that has a round shape.

We can also divide Earth from pole to pole by imagining a line that goes through the poles and that crosses the equator at two points. This line is called the **prime meridian.** It divides Earth into an Eastern Hemisphere and a Western Hemisphere.

Now look at the maps on the left. They show what is in each of the four hemispheres.

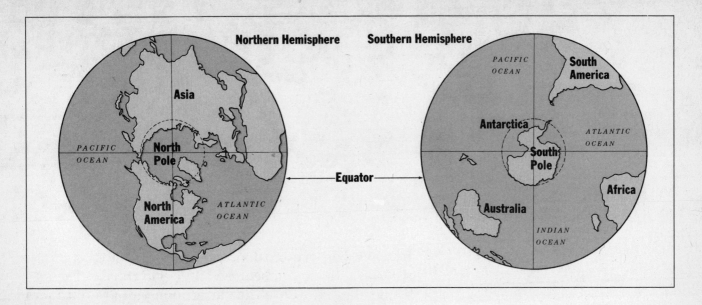

1. Which of the two hemispheres shown above has more water than land?

2. Which hemisphere do you live in?

3. What is the name of the line that divides these two hemispheres?

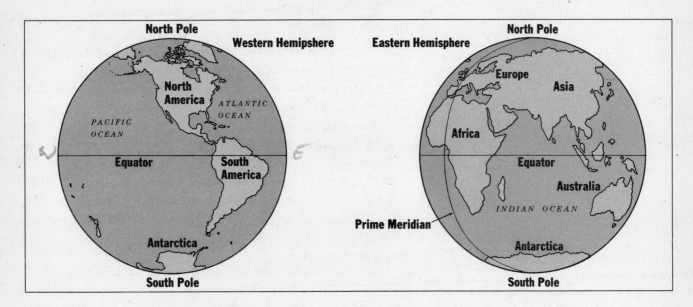

4. Which of the two hemispheres shown above has the most land?

5. Which of these hemispheres do you think has the most people?

6. Which of these hemispheres do you live in?

7. What is the name of the line that divides these two hemispheres?

3

Imagine you are outdoors early in the morning. It is still dark. Soon you see the sun begin to rise. The sun brings daytime. Late that afternoon you are outdoors when the sun begins to set. Slowly the sky grows dark. Soon it is nighttime again.

Why does the sun's light come and go? Does the sun really "rise" and "set"?

Earth Rotates

The sun only **seems** to rise and set. It is Earth's movement, not the sun's, that gives us daytime and nighttime. Earth **rotates,** or spins, all the time. As it rotates, only half of it faces the sun at any time.

In the drawing below, only the Western Hemisphere is getting sunlight. It is daytime there. The other side of the world is in darkness. There it is nighttime.

Now look at the drawing on the next page. The time is 12 hours later. Earth has rotated halfway around. Which hemisphere is now getting sunlight? Which hemisphere is in darkness?

The arrows show the direction in which Earth spins. This drawing shows daytime in the Western Hemisphere.

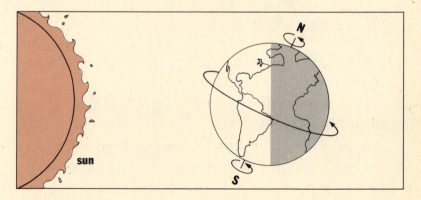

sun

Geography

The Eastern Hemisphere is now getting sunlight. The Western Hemisphere is in darkness.

How long do you think it takes the earth to rotate all the way around?

Earth takes 24 hours to turn completely around. That's why we say that one day is 24 hours long.

Next time you see the sun come up or go down, remember this:

- Daytime comes when the part of Earth you are on moves into sunlight.
- Nighttime comes when the part of Earth you are on moves out of the sunlight.

High-Speed Spin

The Earth rotates at a speed of more than 1,000 miles per hour. Why don't we feel it moving?

We don't feel Earth moving because we are moving along with it. And so is everything else on and near Earth, including the atmosphere.

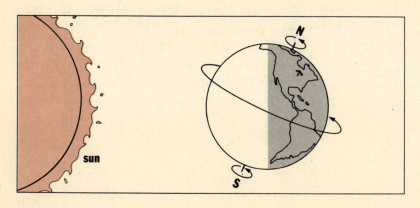

Earth tilts, or leans to one side, as it rotates. This drawing shows nighttime in the Western Hemisphere.

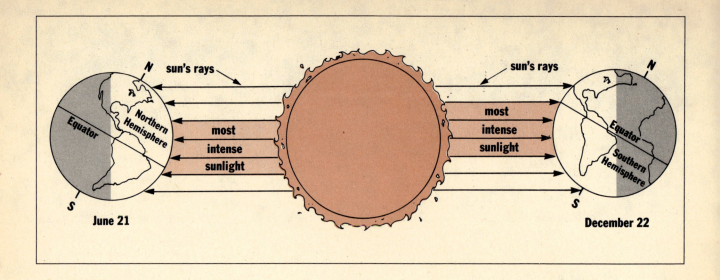

Earth Moves Around the Sun

We said Earth rotates, or spins, and that it makes one complete turn every 24 hours. Earth moves in another way as well. While it is rotating, it is also moving around the sun. Earth takes 365 days to make a complete trip around the sun.

Earth's movement around the sun is what gives us our year. In the time between January 1 and December 31, Earth travels once around the sun.

Earth Is Heated Unevenly

Earth is heated unevenly as it makes its trip around the sun. Some parts of Earth are always warm. Some are always cold. Some parts have small changes in temperature during the year. Other parts have four different **seasons.** They have hot *summers* and cold *winters.* They have warm *springs* and cool *falls.*

The main reason for this uneven heating is the way Earth is tilted. The part of Earth that is directly facing the sun gets hit with intense, or strong, rays of sunlight. That part is warm. The part of Earth tilted away from the sun gets hit with less intense, or weaker, rays of sunlight. That part is cooler.

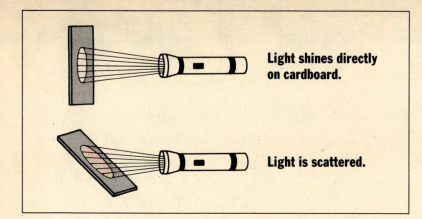

Light shines directly on cardboard.

Light is scattered.

Shine a flashlight on a piece of upright cardboard. Then keep the flashlight in the same place but tilt the cardboard. The light will bounce less intense, or weaker, on the surface of the cardboard. The same thing happens to sunlight hitting Earth.

Look at the drawing above. It shows how light rays are weakened when they shine on a tilted surface.

Now look at the left side of the drawing on page 20. Notice that in late June, the Northern Hemisphere is tilted toward the sun. It is getting more intense sunlight than the Southern Hemisphere. In late June, summer is beginning in the Northern Hemisphere. And winter is beginning in the Southern Hemisphere.

Now look at the right side of the drawing. Which hemisphere is tilted toward the sun in late December?

In late December, the Southern Hemisphere is tilted toward the sun. It is getting more intense sunlight than the Northern Hemisphere. In late December, summer is beginning in the Southern Hemisphere. And winter is beginning in the Northern Hemisphere.

Winter and summer, of course, are not the only seasons. From late March to late June, the light that shines on the Northern Hemisphere is becoming more and more intense. The days are getting warmer. It is springtime. In the Southern Hemisphere, it is fall.

From late September to late December, the light that shines on the Northern Hemisphere is becoming less and less intense. The days are getting cooler. It is fall. In the Southern Hemisphere, it is spring.

At the Poles and the Equator

The areas on and near the equator receive intense sunlight all year long. Most places there are warm to hot all year.

The areas near the poles get little or no sunlight for part of the year. And the sunlight during the rest of the year is not very intense. The temperatures are cool to cold most of the year.

Summary

1. Earth rotates once every 24 hours.
2. Earth moves in a direct path around the sun. The trip takes 365 days.
3. Earth is heated unevenly as it moves around the sun. One reason for this is Earth's tilt.
   - Places on and near the equator get intense sunlight all year. Most places are warm to hot year round.
   - The sunlight that falls on places near the poles is less intense than the sunlight falling anywhere else on Earth. Most places there are cool to cold year round.
   - The sunlight that falls on other parts of Earth becomes more intense and less intense during the course of the year. These places have seasons.

Questions to Discuss

1. What is really happening when you watch a sunrise or sunset?
2. Suppose Earth did not rotate. How would things on Earth be different?
3. Why do some parts of Earth have seasons?

Special Projects

1. Find out why we add an extra day to the month of February every four years.
2. Write a report about seasons. Explain what causes them. Tell how seasons are different from each other. Add drawings, photos, or pictures from magazines to show the changes that take place.
3. Check your newspaper for the time of sunrise and sunset each day. Watch the sun as it rises and sets. Try to understand what is really happening.

Finding Distance on a Map

Suppose you want to know how far it is from one city to another. A map **scale** can help you.

Look at the scale on the map below. It shows how much distance on the map equals 300 miles on land. It also shows shorter distances. Each mark after the 0 adds 50 miles to the mark before it. What does the mark between 200 and 300 stand for?

That mark stands for 250 miles. Now suppose that you want to find the distance between the cities of Tampa and Miami in Florida. Here is what to do:

1. Take a piece of paper and place it next to the dots that stand for Tampa and Miami. Mark dots on your paper next to the dots on the map.

2. Line up the dots on your paper with the marks on the scale. Use the scale to see how many miles the distance between your dots stands for.

Look at the drawing below. The scale shows that the distance from Tampa to Miami is 200 miles.

Now find the distance between these cities:

1. Dallas and Houston (TX)
2. Atlanta and Macon (GA)
3. Birmingham (AL) and Charleston (SC)

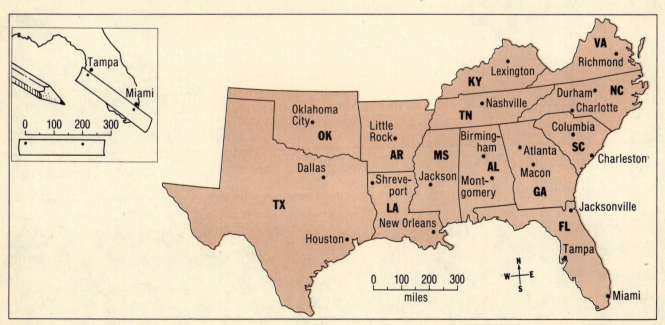

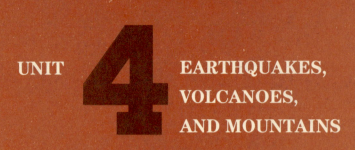

Picture yourself shopping in a supermarket. Suddenly the building begins to sway. Apples and oranges roll out of their bins. Cans and jars tumble from the shelves.

What's going on?

It's an **earthquake.**

Results of the 1906 San Francisco earthquake.

What Causes Earthquakes?

Earth's crust is made of rocks. Every day, some of these rocks shift or break below Earth's surface. This movement causes earthquakes.

Most earthquakes are too weak for us to feel. But strong earthquakes can destroy buildings, bridges, and highways.

The two parts of this fence were joined together before the 1906 San Francisco earthquake.

Up, Down, and Sideways

During an earthquake, the ground may move up or down. Or it may move sideways. The movement can shake buildings apart.

When the ground moves down, buildings sink with it. When the ground moves sideways, anything built on it may be torn apart. Part of a fence or highway may be moved away from another part.

We can't tell exactly where or when an earthquake will happen. But scientists have a good idea of where they are *likely* to happen. And scientists are working on ways to tell when they will happen.

The scientists use very sensitive machines to keep track of every earthquake. The machines are called **seismographs.** A seismograph can record even very small movements within Earth's crust.

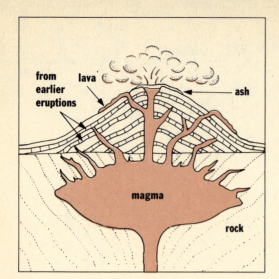

Volcanoes Release Pressure

Imagine that you are sleeping. Suddenly you are awakened by a loud roar. You rush to a window and look out. Huge flames and great clouds of smoke and ash are rising into the air. Something hot and thick is oozing out over the ground. You are watching the eruption of a **volcano.**

What Causes Volcanoes?

Remember, part of the mantle, the layer below Earth's crust, is made of super hot melted rock. This rock is called **magma.**

Some of the magma melts openings in the solid rock of the crust above it. Magma rises up through the openings and forms large pools under Earth's surface.

The weight of the solid rock around the pools presses on the magma. This causes the magma either to melt or to blast openings in the weak parts of the rock. The magma then pushes its way through the openings to the surface.

When the magma erupts onto the surface, it flows over the land. If the eruption is a strong one, smoke and ash can rise high into the sky. Winds may carry the ash far away before it falls to the ground.

After magma erupts, we call it **lava.** The lava cools and hardens into solid rock.

Once a volcano starts, it may go on erupting for a long time. Or it may stop erupting and then erupt again many years later.

Volcanoes Build Mountains

What do you think happens when a volcano erupts again and again, building up layers of lava?

Over long periods of time, the layers of hardened lava become mountains. A mountain thousands of feet high may take thousands of years to build.

Mount Saint Helens in Washington began erupting about 40,000 years ago. In 1980 it erupted with such force that it blew away part of it's top. The mountain became shorter than it was before the eruption. However, if it keeps on erupting it will build a new top.

Lava eruption.

Sometimes the magma does not break through the crust. Sometimes it just pushes the crust upward. This action forms dome mountains. The Black Hills of South Dakota are dome mountains.

Volcanoes often erupt below the ocean floor. When that happens, the layers of lava may rise above the water and form islands. Hawaii was formed in this way.

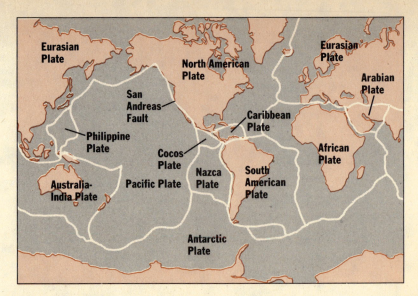

Plates and Earthquakes

Slipping and breaking rock in Earth's crust causes earthquakes. But what causes the rocks to slip or break?

Here is what many scientists think is happening.

Scientists say that Earth's crust is made of a number of **plates.** The continents and oceans sit on these plates. And the plates "float" on Earth's mantle.

The plates are always moving. Some plates move toward each other. Some move apart. Some plates scrape past each other.

Scientists are not sure *why* the plates move. But they are quite sure the plates do move. They say the plates move between half an inch and four inches a year.

That may not seem like very much. But over millions of years, this movement causes great changes on Earth's surface.

Plates Put Pressure on Rocks

When two plates scrape past or press against each other for a long time, pressure builds up on the rocks of each plate. The pressure causes rock to suddenly slip or break. And this causes an earthquake.

Most earthquakes happen where there are **faults,** or deep cracks, in Earth's crust. The faults were also caused by the pressure of plate movement.

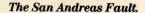

Most faults lie beneath Earth's surface and can't be seen. But some, such as the 600-mile-long San Andreas Fault in California, can be seen from the air.

Far below the San Andreas Fault are the edges of the Pacific and the North American plates. The Pacific Plate is slowly moving north of the North American Plate.

Part of the California coast sits on the Pacific Plate. What do you think is happening to that part of the coast?

That part of the California coast is moving toward Alaska! It is moving about two inches a year.

There are many earthquakes along the San Andreas and other nearby faults. A 1906 earthquake almost destroyed San Francisco. The Los Angeles area has had some bad earthquakes in recent times. And small earthquakes are felt along the San Andreas Fault every year.

Undersea volcanic eruption.

Three Kinds of Mountains

Scientists say there are three main kinds of mountains. They are volcanic, folded, and block mountains.

Volcanic Mountains

You have already read about how volcanoes can build mountains. But the first step in starting most volcanoes is plate movement.

When two plates collide, the edge of one may slide under the edge of the other. The lower edge sinks into Earth's hot mantle. Rocks in the sinking edge are melted by the heat and become new magma. The new, lighter magma rises upward. Some of it breaks through Earth's crust. It forms the kind of volcanic mountains you read about earlier.

Some volcanic mountains form under the ocean. This happens when plates carrying parts of the ocean floor move away from each other, leaving an opening in

Earth's crust. Magma from the mantle rises up through the opening and becomes lava.

The lava spreads out on the ocean floor and hardens into new crust. Over millions of years, the oceans grow wider.

In some places, the lava builds up into underwater mountains. The Mid-Atlantic Ridge is a chain of volcanic mountains that lies under the Atlantic Ocean. The tops of some of the higher mountains rise up above the water as islands.

The Sierra Nevadas.

Folded Mountains

When two plates collide, they press against each other for millions of years. This pressure can cause layers of rock on each plate to bend and fold into mountains and valleys. The high parts are called folded mountains. Scientists believe that the Appalachian Mountains were formed this way.

Block Mountains

Some parts of Earth's crust have many faults. Sometimes, layers of rock between these faults break into huge blocks. Later, some of the blocks get pushed up and form mountains. Scientists believe that the Sierra Nevadas were formed in this way.

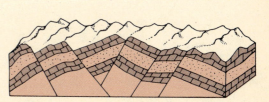

Earthquakes, Volcanoes, and Mountains

Summary

1. Scientists believe that Earth's crust is made of a number of huge plates. The continents and oceans sit on these plates.

2. The plates move from half an inch to four inches every year. Sometimes the plates collide or scrape past each other. This pressure causes faults, or deep cracks, in Earth's crust. The pressure also causes rocks along the faults to slip or break. This slipping and breaking of rocks causes earthquakes.

3. Sometimes one plate slides under another plate. Rocks in the lower plate melt as the lower plate sinks into Earth's mantle. This adds more magma, or melted rock, to the mantle.

4. The new, lighter magma rises up through Earth's crust. It may erupt and form volcanoes and volcanic mountains, both on land and in the oceans. Or it may push the crust upward and form dome mountains.

5. Movement in Earth's crust also leads to the formation of folded mountains and block mountains.

Questions to Discuss

1. What is an earthquake and what causes it?

2. What is a volcano and what causes it?

3. How is each of these kinds of mountains formed?
   - volcanic   - folded   - block

4. How do you think earthquakes and volcanoes affect people's lives?

Special Projects

1. Ask your librarian to help you find newspaper and magazine stories about earthquakes and volcanoes that have taken place in recent years. Write a report or tell the class about one or more of these events.

2. Do you live on or near a mountain? If so, find out how the mountain was formed.

Reading a Table

Tables often give useful information. Table 1 gives facts about some earthquakes. These earthquakes happened in North America between 1964 and 1987.

This table also shows how strong each earthquake was. Earthquakes are measured on a scale of one to ten. An earthquake that measures six or more can destroy some buildings and roads. An earthquake that measures eight or more can destroy a town or large parts of a city.

Table 2 gives facts about some volcanoes. These volcanoes erupted in the United States between 1984 and 1986.

Now see what you can learn from the tables.

Table 1 Earthquakes

1. Which state had an earthquake in 1964?

2. How strong was it?

3. Which country had a 7.5 earthquake in 1976?

4. Which two earthquakes were the strongest?

Table 2 Volcanoes

1. Which three states have volcanoes that erupted in 1986?

2. What are the names of the two Hawaiian volcanoes on the list?

3. Which of them erupted in 1984?

4. Which state had the most eruptions from 1984 to 1986?

Table 1

Strong Earthquakes in North America 1964–1987		
YEAR	PLACE	STRENGTH
1964	Alaska	8.5
1971	California	6.5
1976	Guatemala	7.5
1985	Mexico City	8.1
1987	California	6.6
1987	Alaska	7.4

Table 2

Some Eruptions of U.S. Volcanoes 1984–1986		
YEAR	VOLCANO	PLACE
1984	Mauna Loa	Hawaii
1984	Veniaminof	Alaska
1984	Pavlof	Alaska
1986	Mount Saint Helens	Washington
1986	Kilauea	Hawaii
1986	Augustine	Alaska

5

OTHER FORCES THAT CHANGE EARTH

You know how plate action and volcanoes help build mountains. Other forces wear down those mountains and make other changes on Earth's surface. These forces include water, wind, ice, and people.

Wearing Down Rock

Mountains are made of different kinds of rock. Some of these rocks are harder than others. But in time all can be softened and broken up. This is called **weathering.** It goes on above and below ground.

Some weathering is caused by the action of chemicals on the rock. The chemicals are in the water that falls as rain or that seeps down through the ground. The chemicals are also in streams and rivers that flow over rocks.

The chemicals weaken or soften the rocks. Some rocks break apart. Some dissolve in the water.

Rocks are worn down in other ways, too. Steady, heavy rains wear holes in softer rocks. The rocks begin to break apart.

Sometimes rain fills cracks in rocks. During cold weather, the rainwater freezes. Freezing water expands, cracking the rocks apart.

This rockface shows the effects of weathering. These hikers are sitting under a natural bridge formed by rain and wind.

Things to Find Out

1. How Earth's surface is changed by water, ice, and wind
2. Some ways people change Earth's surface

Water Erosion

Streams break down weathered rock and then carry it away. This is called water **erosion.** Erosion is the carrying away of weathered rock. Fast-moving water slams one rock into another. Rocks are broken down into stones and stones into sand.

Streams twist and turn and wear away **soil** from their banks. Soil is very fine bits of weathered rock mixed with living matter and the remains of plants and animals. The rock, stones, sand, and soil carried by streams are called **sediment.** The streams run into rivers, carrying the sediment with them. Rivers flow across the land and they, too, wear away sand and soil and gather sediment.

When a river reaches flatter land, it slows down. The sediment begins to drop out. First the heavy rocks fall. Then the stones, sand, and soil drop out.

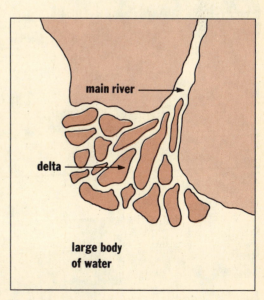

Deltas often form where a river flows into a lake or ocean.

Some sediment builds up new river banks. Some builds sandbars and even islands. An area with a number of islands built from sediment is called a **delta.**

Most river sediment is carried out to the ocean. There it sinks to the ocean floor.

In time, weathering and erosion can greatly change the shape of the land.

Wearing Down Plateaus

Water also erodes plateaus. Rocks become weathered and broken down by rivers that carry them away.

The Grand **Canyon** in Arizona is an example of this. Over millions of years, the Colorado River has carved out steep valleys in the Colorado Plateau. The valleys are a mile deep in some places.

The Grand Canyon.

Wave Erosion

Every day, waves full of sand and stone pound against ocean shores. Where there are high cliffs, the waves can break away pieces of the cliffs and cut out caves at the bottom of them. This weakens the cliffs. Sometimes large parts of them fall away into the ocean.

Waves also wear rock down into sand, making sandy beaches. Sand can come from the sediment brought down by rivers, too.

When water from a breaking wave rolls up onto a beach, it carries some sand with it. When the water rolls back, it takes some sand away. If the amount of sand taken away is the same as the amount brought in, the beach remains about the same size.

But during winter storms, the waves are larger than usual. They wash away more sand than they bring in. In time, a beach may be washed away.

In the summertime, gentle waves leave more sand than they take away. That's why beaches look wider in summer.

Wind Erosion

Wind, too, can erode parts of Earth. In farmlands, wind blows away soil that has been loosened by plowing and dry weather. In desert and beach areas wind blows the loose sand around. It builds and moves sand **dunes.**

Fine bits of soil can be moved by even light winds. Strong winds remove far more soil. In some places, huge dust storms may blacken the daytime sky.

The soil may fall back to Earth far from where it was picked up. Over thousands of years, deep layers of wind-carried soil may form where the wind has carried it.

Much of America's corn is grown in wind-carried soil on the plains of Kansas, Iowa, and Illinois. Wheat is grown on wind-carried soil in Kansas, Nebraska, and Washington.

Wave erosion formed the cave in the base of this cliff.

Erosion by Glaciers

Thousands of years ago, the temperatures in some places were much lower than they are today. In most of northern Asia, Europe, and North America, the snow didn't melt even in the summer. The same was true for the snow in high mountain areas elsewhere on Earth.

Layers of snow built up over thousands of years. Tons of snow pressed down on the lower layers. These lower layers turned to ice, and then the huge bodies of ice and snow began to move. We call these bodies of ice and snow **glaciers.**

Some of the glaciers moved *very* slowly. Some moved as much as 30 feet a day. As they moved, they scraped or pushed at the rock and soil.

Glaciers that moved down mountains scraped away the sides of the mountains. They widened valleys. Most glaciers carried big rocks and great amounts of soil with them. As the rocks moved they sometimes scooped out great chunks of land.

When the glaciers began to melt, they often left hills of rock and soil behind them. Water from the melting glaciers filled some of the scooped-out places and formed lakes. The Greak Lakes were made in this way. In some places, the land was rubbed smooth by the passing glaciers.

Today, glaciers still form where snow does not melt from year to year. There are glaciers in Alaska, in places close to the North and South poles, and on the tops of many high mountains.

A glacier in Alaska

Erosion by People

Tree cutting, overuse of the soil, strip mining, and building roads and houses on hillsides are some of the ways people cause erosion.

We've been cutting down trees for thousands of years. We do it to clear the land for building and farming. We do it to get wood for **fuel** and for lumber and other wood products.

What do you think happens to a hillside when all its trees are cut down?

Trees break the force of raindrops. Fallen leaves soak up much of the water from rainfall and melting snow. When the trees are cut down, the soil and fallen leaves wash away. Nothing is left to soak up the water. The soil turns to mud that may then slide downhill. Sometimes houses and other buildings slide down with the mud.

Today, many logging companies plant new trees to replace the ones they've cut down.

Sometimes, farmers cause erosion when they overuse the soil. Planting the same crop year after year can wear out the soil so that crops can't grow in it. Then, in dry, windy weather, the soil may blow away because there are no plants to hold it in place.

Today, most farmers plant different crops from time to time so the soil won't wear out. Or they grow grass, clover, or other nonfood plants on part of their land for awhile. This helps preserve the soil.

Mining companies often cause erosion. They strip away land to get at coal, iron, and other **minerals** buried in the ground. This leaves bare rock and big holes.

Today, some mining companies replace and replant the soil in areas that they've mined.

UNIT REVIEW

Summary

1. Water can weather and erode rock:
   - Chemicals in the water weaken, soften, and dissolve rock.
   - Heavy rain makes holes in some kinds of rock.
   - Water freezes in cracks and expands, breaking the rock apart.
   - Streams break up rock and carry it away.
   - Waves wear down rock and wash away beaches.
2. Rivers form new banks, sandbars, and islands from the sediment they carry.
3. Wind blows away loose sand and soil. It builds sand dunes and moves soil to new places.
4. Glaciers can widen valleys and scoop out lake beds. They may leave behind hills of rock and soil. They may also smooth out the land.
5. People can cause erosion when they cut down trees, overuse the soil, and mine.

Questions to Discuss

1. What are some ways that each of the following can change the land?
   - water   • wind   • glaciers   • people
2. Think about where you live and the areas nearby. How have water, wind, and people affected landforms there? What changes are they making now?

Special Projects

1. Imagine you are a million years old. Tell a story about how your favorite mountain was formed and how it was worn down by weathering and erosion.
2. Go out and look at the land around you. Visit a stream, river, lake, or ocean beach. Look for signs of changes made by water, wind, and people. Draw or take pictures of what you see. Write captions for your pictures. Display your work in class.
3. Find out about the last Ice Age, when glaciers covered much of North America. Report to the class.

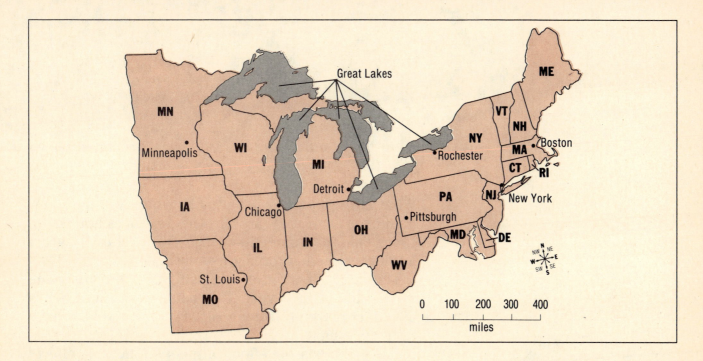

Finding "In-Between" Directions

We do not always move directly north, south, east, or west. Sometimes we move in a direction that is in between these directions. Look at the map above. Find St. Louis, Missouri, and Chicago, Illinois. If you were to fly from St. Louis to Chicago, in which direction would you be flying?

You would be flying both north and east. That is, you would be flying northeast.

The compass rose on the left of the map can help you figure out "in-between" directions. Here is what the "in-between" letters stand for:

NE: northeast   NW: northwest
SE: southeast   SW: southwest

Now imagine flying between the following cities. In which direction do you fly:

1. Chicago (IL) to St. Louis (MO)?
2. Minneapolis (MN) to Chicago (IL)?
3. Pittsburg (PA) to Detroit (MI)?
4. New York (NY) to Boston (MA)?

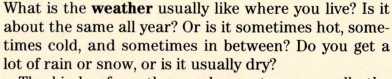

UNIT 6 EARTH'S DIFFERENT CLIMATES

What is the **weather** usually like where you live? Is it about the same all year? Or is it sometimes hot, sometimes cold, and sometimes in between? Do you get a lot of rain or snow, or is it usually dry?

The kinds of weather a place gets are usually the same from year to year. This usual yearly weather is called **climate.** Different places in the world have different climates.

Climate has a big effect on people's lives. It affects the kinds of food they can grow. It affects the kinds of clothing they wear. It affects the kinds of houses they live in. What else might it affect?

Did you think about the kind of outdoor activities they can enjoy?

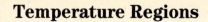

Temperature Regions

Several things affect air temperature where you live. They include:

- intensity of sunlight
- nearness to large bodies of water
- **elevation**
- wind

In this unit, we will look at each of these. Let's start with the first one, intensity of sunlight.

There are three main temperature **regions** on Earth. A region is a group of places that have one or more things that are alike.

Things to Find Out

1. What climate is
2. How and why climates are different in different places

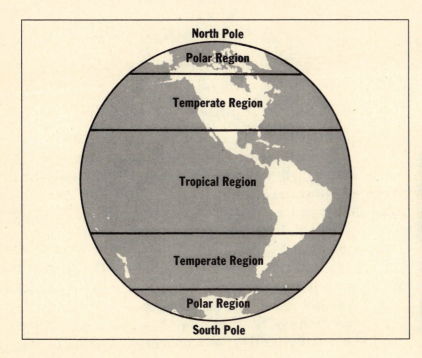

The lines running east and west show where each temperature region begins and ends. What are the names of the three regions? Which region is North America in?

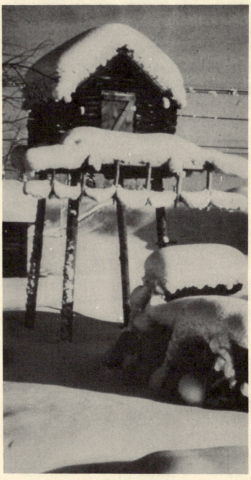

In a temperature region, most places in the region have similar temperatures. This is because the sunlight falls with about the same intensity everywhere in the region.

The temperature of most places in the tropical region is usually warm to hot.

The temperature of most places in the two polar regions is usually cold to very cold.

The temperature of most places in the two temperate regions changes as Earth moves around the sun. It is usually cool to cold in winter. It is usually warm to hot in summer.

In summer, warm air over the coast rises up. Cooler air from over the ocean takes its place. This helps keep coastal temperatures lower than those farther inland.

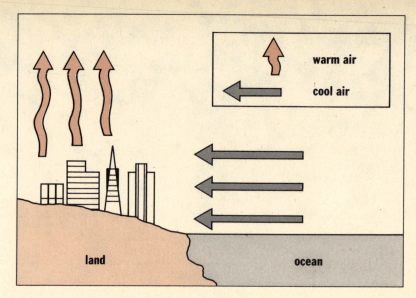

warm air

cool air

land

ocean

Oceans Affect Temperature

Large bodies of water can help raise or lower air temperature over nearby lands. Here is an example.

Kansas City, Missouri, and San Francisco, California, both get about the same intensity of sunlight. But San Francisco is much warmer in the winter than Kansas City. And San Francisco is cooler in the summer.

Kansas City is far from any ocean. But San Francisco is next to the Pacific Ocean. Oceans and other large bodies of water take longer to warm up than land does. They also take longer to cool off.

In winter, the ocean near San Francisco is warmer than the nearby land. The ocean helps warm the air over the land.

In summer, the ocean near San Francisco is colder than the nearby land. The ocean helps to cool the air over the land.

Ocean Currents

There is another way that oceans affect temperatures along a coast. Cool ocean water flows from cool regions to warm regions. Warm ocean water flows from warm regions to cool regions. The water flows in currents that are like giant streams within the oceans.

Winds passing over the currents are either heated or cooled. Later, when these winds pass over a coastal area, they heat or cool the land there.

Elevation Affects Temperature

Have you ever hiked up a mountain? If so, you may have felt the air get cooler as you climbed higher. This happens everywhere, even in the hot tropics.

For each 1,000 feet you climb above sea level, the temperature drops about 3½ degrees Fahrenheit.

Suppose it is 80° F at the foot of a mountain. People there might wear T-shirts and shorts to play a game of volleyball.

About 8,000 feet up the mountain, the temperature may drop to 52° F. Hikers need warm shirts to be comfortable there.

At the same time, the temperature at 15,000 feet may be only 27° F. Mountain climbers have to bundle up in parkas to keep out the cold.

15,000 feet
27° F

8,000 feet
52° F

sea level
80° F

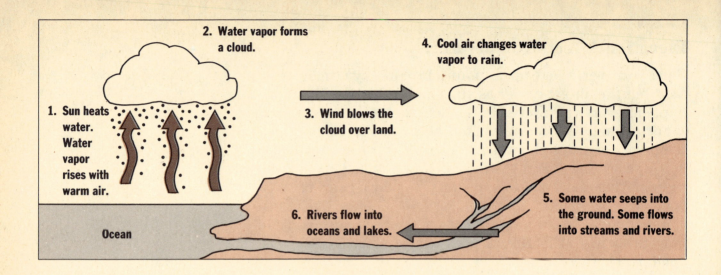

1. Sun heats water. Water vapor rises with warm air.

2. Water vapor forms a cloud.

3. Wind blows the cloud over land.

4. Cool air changes water vapor to rain.

5. Some water seeps into the ground. Some flows into streams and rivers.

6. Rivers flow into oceans and lakes.

Ocean

Precipitation

Rain, snow, sleet, and hail are all forms of **precipitation**. Where does this wet stuff come from?

The sun beats down on Earth's lakes and oceans. The water begins to **evaporate**. It turns into a gas called water vapor. Plants and soil also give off water vapor when they are heated by the sun.

When the heated air rises, the water vapor rises up with it. As the air rises, it starts to cool down. Cool air can't hold as much water vapor as warm air can. The water vapor mixes with tiny bits of dust and other matter in the air and forms into droplets of water. The droplets form clouds.

What Makes the Drops Fall?

If there is a lot of **moisture** and the air continues to cool, the droplets in the clouds come together and form larger drops. If the drops become heavier than the air, they start falling to the ground.

When the air is not too cold, the drops fall as rain. If the temperature of the air is below freezing (32° F), the drops falls as snow, sleet, or hail. Sleet is frozen raindrops. Hail is balls of ice. The balls are usually small. But sometimes they can be as large as baseballs.

Some of the water that falls soaks into the ground. But much of it flows into streams and rivers. The rivers flow into lakes and oceans.

In this way, Earth's water moves in an endless cycle. A cycle is something that goes around and around.

Different places on Earth get different amounts of precipitation. Some deserts get no precipitation at all. Some tropical forests get over 400 inches per year.

Winds

Heated air rises, cooler air moves in to take its place. This movement of air is what makes wind.

Winds blow across the continents and oceans every day. When wind from a cool place passes over a warmer place, it lowers the temperature there. When wind from a warmer place passes over a cooler place, it raises the temperature.

Winds also affect precipitation. They carry water vapor and storms from one place to another.

Windstorms

Hurricanes are strong storms with wind speeds that sometimes reach 150 miles per hour. They usually start over oceans. Then they may move inland. Often they carry much rain with them.

Hurricanes sink ships. They whip up huge waves that wash away beaches. They blow away trees and houses.

Tornados start over land. They move quickly over small areas. They toss cars and trucks about as if they were toys. They destroy houses and other buildings.

One side of a mountain may get more precipitation than the others.

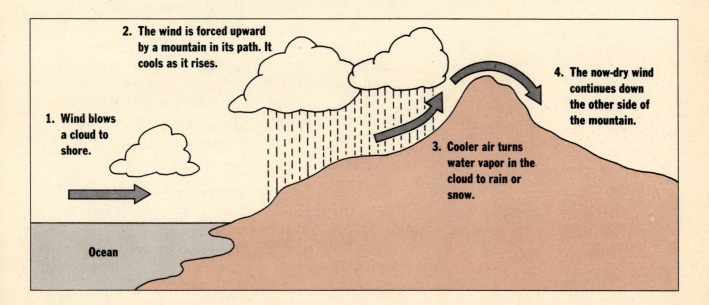

1. Wind blows a cloud to shore.

2. The wind is forced upward by a mountain in its path. It cools as it rises.

3. Cooler air turns water vapor in the cloud to rain or snow.

4. The now-dry wind continues down the other side of the mountain.

Ocean

Three Different Kinds of Climate

You have been reading about different things that can
affect the climate of a place. Read now how these
things affect the climate of three different places in
the United States.

North Coast of Alaska: Polar

The north coast of Alaska is in the polar region. The
sunlight there is much less intense than places farther
south. The ocean waters nearby are frozen over for
most of the year. Sea winds blowing over the land are
cold.

Winters are long and bitterly cold. Temperatures
often drop well below 0° F.

Summers are short and cool. Summer temperatures
seldom go above 50° F.

Summer days are long. But the intensity of the
sunlight is weak. The ground below the surface stays
frozen all year. Only tiny plants are able to grow.

The air is usually so cold it cannot hold much water
vapor. In the town of Barrow, only about five inches of
precipitation fall each year.

Kansas: Continental

Kansas is in the temperate region. The intensity of the
sunlight there changes during the year. There are no
large bodies of water nearby to affect temperatures.

As you have probably guessed, Kansas has fairly cold
winters and warm summers. Usual temperatures range
from about 31° F in winter to about 79° F in July.

The eastern part of the state gets about 35 inches of precipitation a year, while the western part gets only about 18 inches. Most of the state's precipitation comes as spring and summer rains.

Winds blowing in from the west help keep the air clean of pollution. Kansas sometimes gets tornadoes.

Florida: Subtropical

Florida does not have the cold winters that states farther north have. It is closer to the equator. So the sunlight it gets is more intense. But it is also a peninsula, with water on three sides.

The water helps warm the state in winter and cool it in summer. Usual temperatures range from about 59° F in January to about 81° F in July.

Temperatures throughout the state seldom drop below 50° F. But sometimes, in the northern parts of the state, temperatures may drop below freezing.

Florida gets quite a bit of rain, about 53 inches a year. This happens because the intense sunlight over the area evaporates a lot of water from the nearby Gulf of Mexico. The water vapor rises in the warm air. When it reaches the cooler upper air, it forms clouds and turns to rain.

Most of the rain falls with the hurricanes that happen in late summer and fall. Hurricane winds sometimes reach speeds of over 150 miles an hour.

Miami, Florida, is warm most of the year.

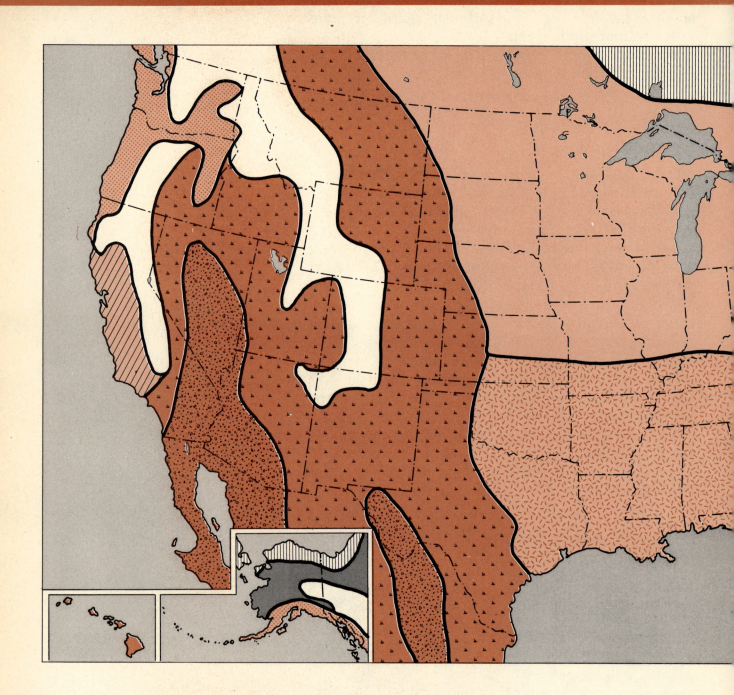

Reading a Climate Map

The map above shows climate regions in the United States. Each region is marked with a different shading or marking.

The key tells what each shading or marking stands for. For example, this stands for a climate that is warm to cool and sometimes wet: ▨

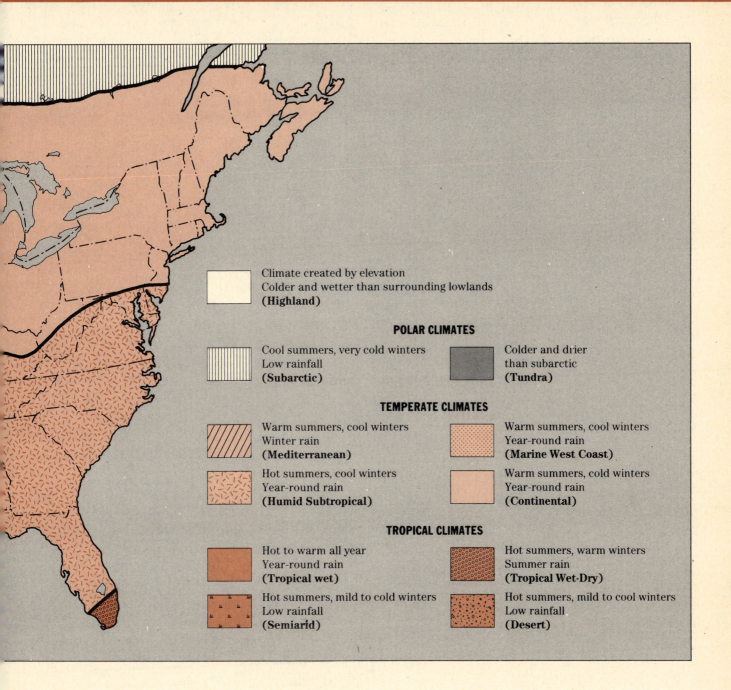

Climate created by elevation
Colder and wetter than surrounding lowlands
(Highland)

POLAR CLIMATES

Cool summers, very cold winters
Low rainfall
(Subarctic)

Colder and drier
than subarctic
(Tundra)

TEMPERATE CLIMATES

Warm summers, cool winters
Winter rain
(Mediterranean)

Warm summers, cool winters
Year-round rain
(Marine West Coast)

Hot summers, cool winters
Year-round rain
(Humid Subtropical)

Warm summers, cold winters
Year-round rain
(Continental)

TROPICAL CLIMATES

Hot to warm all year
Year-round rain
(Tropical wet)

Hot summers, warm winters
Summer rain
(Tropical Wet-Dry)

Hot summers, mild to cold winters
Low rainfall
(Semiarid)

Hot summers, mild to cool winters
Low rainfall
(Desert)

Highland climates depend on elevation. They may also depend on which side of a mountain a place is on.

Study the map and key. What is the climate like in your part of the country?

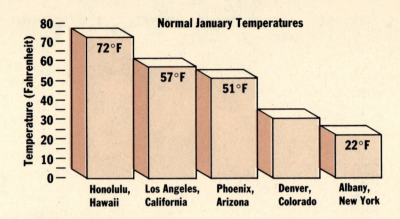

Reading a Bar Graph

A bar graph can give you a quick way to compare amounts. The bar graph above compares normal January temperatures in five different cities.

The numbers on the left show temperatures from 0° F to 80° F. The marks between two numbers stand for numbers halfway between those numbers. The mark between 10 and 20 stands for 15. What does the mark between 50 and 60 stand for?

Each bar shows the normal January temperature in the city named below the bar. The number at the top of the bar tells what that temperature is.

What is the normal January temperature in Los Angeles?

If the number is not printed at the top of the bar, you can still tell what the number should be. Use a ruler or piece of paper to help you. Place the ruler so that its bottom edge runs from the top of the bar to the numbers on the left—like this:

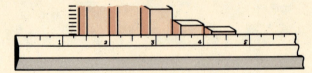

Now answer these questions:

1. What is the normal January temperature in Denver?
2. What is the normal January temperature in Albany?
3. Which of the five cities is warmest in January?
4. Which two cities have normal January temperatures that are below freezing?

Summary

1. The climate of a place is its usual yearly weather.
2. Five things may affect the climate of a place.
   - how intensely the sun's rays shine on it
   - how close it is to a large body of water
   - the temperature of any nearby ocean currents
   - how high it is above sea level
   - where the winds that pass overhead come from
3. The water cycle starts with the sun's evaporating water from Earth's surface. Rising water vapor forms clouds. Water from the clouds returns to Earth as rain, snow, sleet, or hail.
4. The climates in different parts of the United States can be quite different.

Questions to Discuss

1. What is the climate like where you live? Talk about temperature, precipitation, and winds. Give some reasons why the climate is the way it is.
2. How does your climate affect:
   - the kind of clothes you wear?
   - the kind of building you live in?
   - the kinds of outdoor things you can do?

Special Projects

1. Choose one of the places described on pages 48–49. Draw a travel poster that tells something about the climate of the place. Or write an ad about the place. Try to make people want to visit or live there.
2. Learn and report about two states that have very different climates. You might compare Alaska and Hawaii, Florida and Maine, or Minnesota and Arizona. List the reasons these places have such different climates. Report to the class.

UNIT **7** VEGETATION AND SOILS

Vegetation Types

Some plants need a lot of warmth and water. Others need much less. So climate affects the **vegetation**, or kinds of plants, that grow in a place.

The main types of vegetation are forest, grassland, **tundra,** desert, and highland. To learn about them, let's visit some different states.

Things to Find Out

1. The main types of *vegetation* on Earth
2. The affect of climate on vegetation
3. How soil is formed and what plants get from it

***Vegetation:* Needleleaf Forest**
***State:* Maine**

The forests of northern Maine have mostly needleleaf trees. Needleleaf trees have long thin pointed leaves that look like needles. These trees stay green all year.

Needleleaf trees grow mostly in climate regions that have cool to cold winters. They are often found on high cool mountains. But they also grow in warmer places. They can grow well in poor soils.

***Vegetation:* Mixed Forests**
***State:* West Virginia**

Both needleleaf and **broadleaf** trees grow in West Virginia. Different broadleaf trees have flat leaves of different sizes. In places with warm summers and cold winters, broadleaf trees lose their leaves in fall when the weather gets cool. They grow new leaves in spring when the weather warms up again.

***Vegetation:* Tropical Broadleaf Forests**
***State:* Hawaii**

In parts of Hawaii that are warm and wet most of the year, there are thick tropical broadleaf forests. The trees there stay green all year.

***Vegetation:* Scrub Forests**
***State:* California**

Southern California is too dry for forests of large trees. But it does get enough rain for scrub forests to grow.

Scrub forests have short scrub trees with thick bark and waxy leaves. These trees do well in climates that are warm and dry for most of the year.

Hawaii

Vegetation and Soils

Vegetation: Grasslands
States: Nebraska, Iowa, and Florida

Parts of Nebraska and Iowa are covered by grasslands with few if any trees. Most of Nebraska's grasslands are called **steppes.** Steppes have short grass. Most of Iowa's grasslands are called **prairies.** Prairies have tall grass. Steppes and prairies are found where the climate is cool to cold and mostly dry.

Parts of southern Florida have grasslands called **savannas.** Along with the grass, savannas have some widely spaced trees and shrubs. They are found in warm climates that have both wet and dry seasons.

Vegetation: Tundra
State: Alaska

The cold, dry, almost bare land of the north coast of Alaska is a tundra. Very little grows there other than low bushes and small plants. During the short summer, tiny flowers bloom for awhile.

Prairie planted in wheat.

Vegetation: Desert
State: Arizona

If you drive through Arizona, you will see mainly thorny scrubs and cacti. Their hard outer parts help them store water. That's important for desert plants. Deserts get ten or fewer inches of rain a year. Only plants that need little water can grow there.

Vegetation: Highland
State: Idaho

Different kinds of vegetation can be found on the same mountain. On the side that gets enough rain, broadleaf trees grow at the lower elevations. Halfway up, there may be mixed forests. At the higher, cooler elevations there may be only needleleaf trees.

If the other side of the mountain gets little rain, it will have no forests at all. It will have only desert vegetation. And at very high elevations, the climate is too cold and dry for any trees to grow.

Tundra

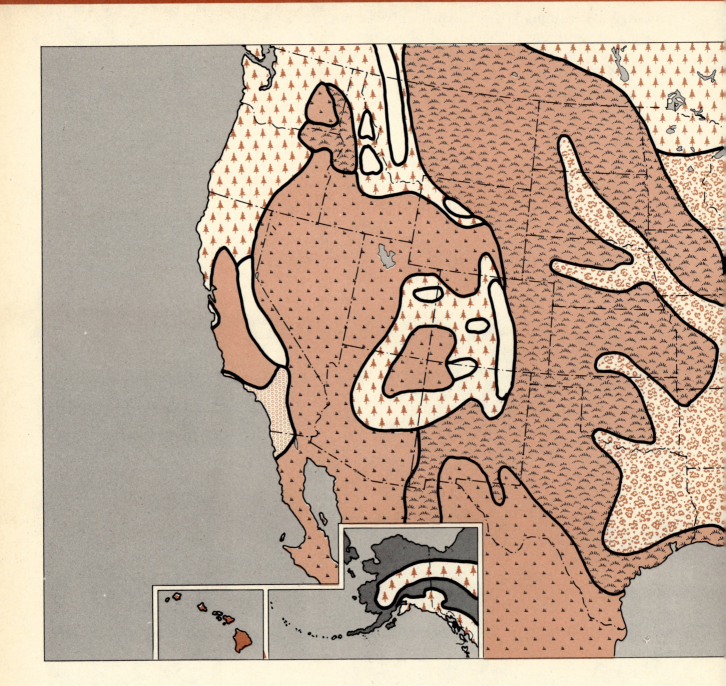

Reading a Vegetation Map

The map above shows vegetation regions in the United States. Each region is marked with a different shading or marking.

The key at the bottom of the map tells what each shading or marking stands for. For example, this stands for needleleaf forests.

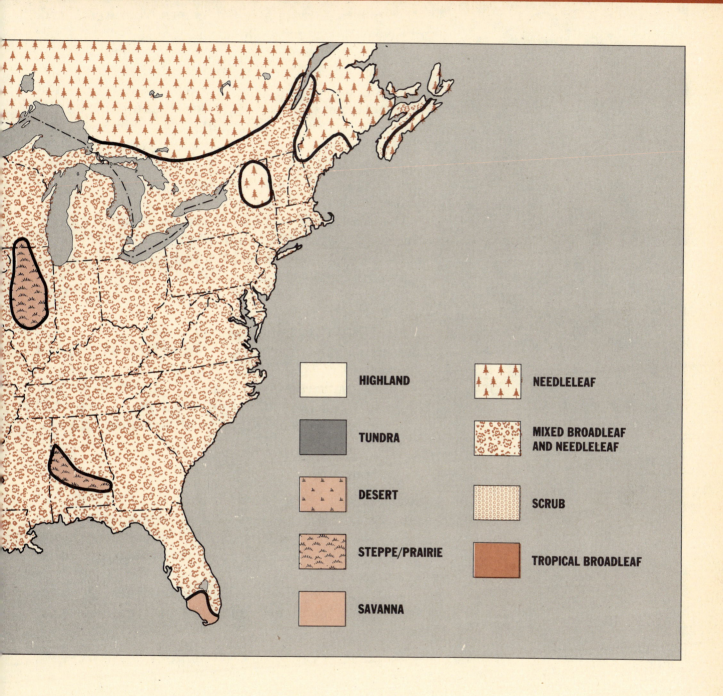

HIGHLAND

NEEDLELEAF

TUNDRA

MIXED BROADLEAF
AND NEEDLELEAF

DESERT

SCRUB

STEPPE/PRAIRIE

TROPICAL BROADLEAF

SAVANNA

Highland vegetation depends on elevation. It may also depend on which side of a mountain or a mountain range a place is on.

Study the map and key. Which vegetation region do you live in?

Vegetation and Soils

Soil

Weathered Rock

Soil

Most plants grow in soil. Soil comes from weathered, or worn down, rock. Rock gets worn down by the action of rain, ice, running water, and chemicals.

Soil is deeper in some places than in others. It ranges from a few inches to many feet deep. But not all land is covered with soil. Some land is bare rock. And some is covered with sand.

Soil contains more than weathered rock. It contains tiny living things too small for us to see without a miscroscope. And it contains the remains of plants and animals that have died.

The dead plant and animal matter is called **humus.** Humus gives plants some of the **nutrients** they need. They get other nutrients from other parts of the soil. Nutrients are the things plants need to grow.

Soil soaks up rainwater and stores it for plants to use.

Plants that do not need much water grow best in sandy soil. Sandy soil is loose. Water passes through it quickly.

Plants that need lots of water grow best in soil that has a lot of clay in it. Clay soil, which gets sticky when wet, holds water longer than sandy soil does.

Farmland Soil

Farmers plant crops that grow best in their climates and on the kinds of soil they have on their farms. Sandy soils are good for root crops like carrots and potatoes. Clay soils are good for wheat and other grains.

If the soil does not have enough nutrients in it, many farmers use **fertilizers**. Fertilizers add nutrients to the soil.

Summary

1. The main types of vegetation are: forest, grassland, tundra, and highland.

2. There are four kinds of forest vegetation: needleleaf, broadleaf, tropical broadleaf, and scrub.

3. Needleleaf trees grow where it is cool or cold in the winter. They stay green all year.

4. In warm climates, broadleaf trees stay green all year. In cooler climates, they lose their leaves in fall and get new ones in spring.

5. Steppes are grasslands with short grass and no trees. They are found in cooler, drier climates.

6. Savannas are grasslands that have some widely spaced trees and shrubs. They are found where it is warm all year and there is a short rainy season.

7. Only low bushes and tiny plants grow on tundras, where the winters are long and bitterly cold.

8. Deserts may have cacti, thorny shrubs, and other plants that need very little water.

9. The vegetation on a mountain changes with the elevation and the amount of precipitation.

10. Soil gives plants the nutrients and water they need.

Questions to Discuss

1. Describe the following kinds of vegetation. Tell how climate affects each one.
   - forest • grassland • desert • tundra
   - highland

2. Which of the five main types of vegetation are found where you live?

3. What kinds of food are grown nearest your home?

Special Projects

1. Cut out pictures of different kinds of vegetation from old magazines. Paste them on paper. Tell what kind of vegetation each picture shows.

2. Collect soil samples from different parts of your town. Plant bean seeds in each sample. See which soils the beans grow best in.

UNIT 8 EARTH'S RENEWABLE RESOURCES

A cave man chipping flint.

What Is a Resource?

Suppose we had no air to breathe or water to drink. What would happen to us?

We would soon die. Air and water are two of Earth's many **resources**. Resources include everything we get from Earth that we need or can use. We call something a resource if we are *able* to make use of it. Sometimes this means having the tools and skills to do that.

Think of rich soil full of nutrients. If no one uses the soil, it is not a resource. But suppose a farmer grows crops in the soil. Then the soil becomes a resource.

Suppose the farmer uses an animal to help with the work. Then the animal is also a resource.

To make use of the soil and the animal, the farmer needs certain tools and skills. What tools and skills do you think a farmer might need?

Our Needs Change

Sometimes we replace one resource with another. Long ago, before people had metal tools, flint was an important resource. Flint is a rock found on Earth's surface. It is easy to chip and shape. People made flint arrowheads, knives, and digging tools.

Then people found out how to make harder, stronger arrowheads and tools from metal. They learned how to get metal from the ground. They learned how to shape it. When they no longer needed flint, they no longer thought of it as an important resource.

At one time, whale oil was an important resource. People burned it in lamps to have light at night. Sailors with special boats and tools hunted for whales all over the world. But when kerosene lamps came into use, whale oil became a much less important resource. Kerosene is made from oil that comes from the ground.

Today, we use **electricity** to light our lamps. Coal, oil, and water power are the main resources we use to produce the electricity.

Renewable Resources

Some resources are renewable. That is, they can be replaced if they are used. Let's see how we use some of our renewable resources.

Energy from the Sun

The sun gives us heat. The heat warms us and helps plants grow.

The sun gives us light. Plants need both warmth and light to grow.

Plants store energy from the sun. Energy is power. When you eat foods made from plants, energy enters your body. It gives you the power to walk, run, and do all the things you do.

The energy stored in oil and coal also came from the sun. You will learn more about that in Unit 9.

Air

Living things need certain gases to stay alive. Plants take in carbon dioxide from the air. They give back oxygen. Animals breathe in the oxygen. They breath out carbon dioxide. The air is like a bank. It holds the gases until they are needed.

Water vapor in the air keeps us from burning up in the daytime and freezing at night. It is also part of the cycle that brings us fresh water.

Water passing through this dam helps make electricity.

Geography

Water

Living things cannot go for long without water. Animals need water to digest food, stay cool, and get rid of wastes. Plants need water to grow.

We use water at home for cooking and cleaning. Farmers use water to raise their crops and keep their animals alive. Some factories use large amounts of water.

Water is also important for travel. Boats carry millions of people up and down rivers and across lakes and oceans. Ships carry millions of tons of goods on Earth's waterways.

Water is used in some places to make electricity. This is done by building a dam across a river to hold back the water. Then some of the water is allowed to flow over the blades of large wheels. The turning wheels drive generators. The generators produce electricity. The electricity is carried over wires to where it will be used.

This sheep's hair will be spun into wool. The wool will be used to make gloves, sweaters, and other warm clothing.

Animals

Think of how important animals are to us.

Do you eat eggs or meat? These come from animals.

Do you drink milk? Milk comes from cows. Butter, cream, and cheese come from milk.

Do you have a sweater, scarf, or anything else made of wool? Wool comes from the hair of sheep.

Do you wear leather shoes or own a leather wallet? Leather comes from the skins of animals.

In some parts of the world, people still hunt to get what they need from animals. But today, most of these needs are met by animals raised on farms and ranches.

In many parts of the world, animals are used to do work. Horses, oxen, and water buffalo pull plows and turn heavy wheels that make flour from grain. Elephants move heavy logs. These animals also carry people and goods from one place to another.

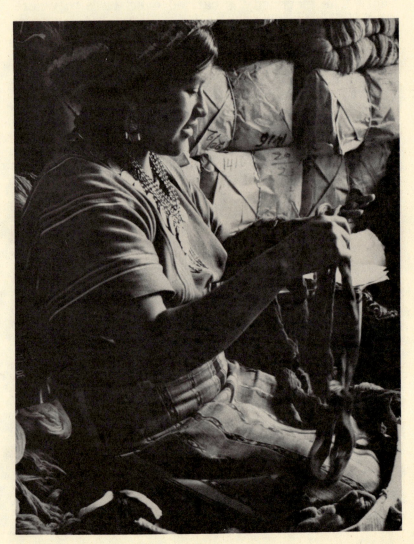

This woman is a member of a wool gathering cooperative in Guatemala.

Fish is an important food for many people. Most of the fish and seafood we eat come from rivers and oceans. But today, fish are also being raised in large ponds on fish farms.

Plants

Plants are our chief source of food. We eat fruits and vegetables. We eat grains like rice, wheat, and corn. And we eat foods made from grains, such as bread and noodles.

We may eat meat from cows, sheep, chickens, and pigs. But all those animals are plant eaters. Without plants, farmers couldn't raise animals.

Some of our clothing comes from plants. Is any of your clothing made of cotton? Cotton comes from the cotton plant.

In warm climates, people may wear straw hats or other clothing made from plants. In some places, people make baskets from parts of plants.

Plants are renewable resources because new plants can be grown to replace those that are used.

Planting rice

Forests

Look around you. How many things do you see that are made of wood? Wood is used to build houses and furniture. It is used to make pencils and rulers. It is ground up to make paper. In many parts of the world, people heat and cook with wood.

Do you have rubber tires on your bike or car? Some rubber comes from the sap of rubber trees.

Some medicines also come from trees.

Forests are very important to us for other reasons. They are home to thousands of kinds of birds and animals. And they are enjoyable places for people to camp, hike, fish, or hunt.

Forests help keep soil from washing or blowing away. They also fill the air with oxygen and water vapor. As we saw earlier, animals need oxygen to breathe. And water vapor is part of the water cycle.

Soil

Soil is one of our most important resources. Trees and other plants grow in it. Most of the world's food comes from plants grown in soil.

Only certain parts of the world have soil that is good for farming. The best farmland is found in valleys and deltas, where rivers have left deep layers of soil. Soil that has just the right mix of nutrients makes the best farmland.

All the resources we have talked about so far are renewable. Some take very little time to replace, such as sunlight, air, and water. Trees take much longer. And it may take hundreds or thousands of years to replace soil that has washed or blown away.

Trees being tapped for rubber.

Summary

1. Resources are things we get from Earth that we need or can use.
2. Renewable resources are resources that can be replaced after they are used.
3. The sun is our chief source of heat, light, and other forms of energy.
4. Air supplies animals with oxygen and plants with carbon dioxide.
5. Water is used for drinking, cooking, cleaning, and watering crops. It is also used in some factories and to make electricity.
6. Animals supply us with both food and clothing.
7. Plants are used for food and to make clothing.
8. Forests may be enjoyed as places to camp, hike, fish, or hunt. Forests supply us with wood, rubber, and other products. They also hold soil in place and fill the air with oxygen and water vapor.

Questions to Discuss

1. What are some renewable resources you use every day? How do you use them? What makes them renewable?
2. Choose one of the resources listed below. Tell how your life would change if that resource were suddenly to disappear.
   - sunlight • air • water • animals • plants
   - forests

Special Projects

Form teams. Find the answers to these questions. Report your answers to the class.

1. Where does your school's water come from? How does it get to the school?
2. Where does your school's electricity come from? How is it produced? How does it get to your school?
3. What kinds of farm crops and animals are raised in your area? Are there any fish farms?

UNIT 9 SOME RESOURCES ARE NOT RENEWABLE

Some natural resources took thousands and even millions of years to form. Once they are used up, they cannot be replaced. We use many of these nonrenewable resources in some way every day.

In this unit, you will read about nonrenewable resources. And you will learn about some of the resource problems we are facing.

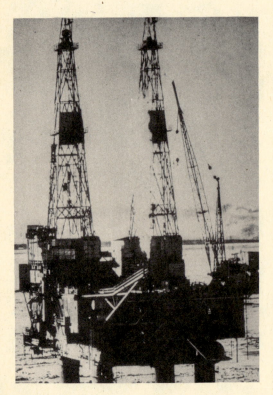

Workers use platforms like this to reach oil buried below the ocean floor.

Nonrenewable Resources

Oil

There has been oil below Earth's surface for millions of years. How did it get there?

Scientists believe the oil was made from the remains of tiny sea plants and animals. When the plants and animals died, they sank to the ocean floor. Layer upon layer of these dead plants and animals were built up. Then they were buried under sediment that came from rivers flowing into the ocean.

The weight of the water and sediment pressed down on the dead matter for millions of years. Scientists say this caused it to turn into oil and natural gas. Later, some of the places that had oil were pushed up above the water. They became dry land. Today, there is oil below both dry land and the ocean's floor.

Special drills are used to get at the oil. The drills are long enough and strong enough to cut through rock.

When the oil is reached, pipes and pumps are used to bring it up to the surface.

What comes out of the ground is a thick black liquid called **crude oil.** Crude oil is used to make heating oil,

Things to Find Out

1. How coal and oil were formed; how we get them out of the ground; how we use them
2. How we get and use other important materials
3. The kinds of resource problems we face and what is being done about them

motor oil, gasoline, plastic, and many other products. It has become one of our most important resources.

Coal

Coal is a black rock that burns slowly and gives off a lot of heat. It is used in factories where steel and other metal products are made.

Coal is also used in some power plants that make electricity. The coal is burned to heat water. The water becomes steam. The steam turns the wheels that drive generators.

Scientists believe it took millions of years for coal to be formed. They say that temperatures were much warmer on Earth millions of years ago. Much of Earth's surface was covered then with muddy land called **swamps.** Large tropical plants grew in these muddy swamps.

When the plants died, they fell into the swamps. In time, the swamps became covered with soil and rock. The soil and rock pressed down on the plant matter for millions of years. It became coal.

Notice that both coal and oil are made mostly from dead plants. While they were living, those plants stored up energy from the sun. So the energy we get from coal and oil really comes from the sun!

Coal is buried below Earth's surface. Workers dig mines to get at the coal.

In some places, the miners dig a shaft, or long deep hole, down to where the coal is. Then they dig tunnels branching out from the shaft.

But most of today's big coal mines are strip mines. Huge machines first strip away the trees and soil. They uncover the coal. Then other huge machines dig it up.

An open pit mine.

The Metals

Coal and oil are minerals that formed from living things. Other minerals were formed in other ways. But they, too, took millions of years to form. And they, too, have to be brought up from out of Earth's crust.

Shaft mines are used to bring up some of these minerals. Strip mines and open pit mines are used to get at others. Open pit mines are like huge holes in the ground big enough for trucks to drive down into.

Minerals are often found mixed together in rock. Many minerals are metals. Rock that contains metal is called **ore.** Miners dig out the ore. Then they remove the metal from it.

Iron, copper, lead, and aluminum are all metals. So are silver and gold. Can you name at least one thing that is made from each of these metals?

Iron is used to make iron fences and other things. But its most important use is in the making of steel. Iron is mixed with other minerals to produce steel. Steel is very strong and lasts for a long time. It is used to build cars, ships, trains, bridges, and large buildings. Some pots, pans, knives, forks, and spoons are also made from steel.

Copper is an important metal. Have you talked on the phone lately? Your voice went out over copper wires. Are there any lights on right now where you are? The electricity is coming in on copper wires. Copper is also used to make water pipes.

Lead is a very heavy metal. Divers use lead weights to help keep them down under water. Lead is also used to make fishing weights and the small weights that balance car wheels. Lead has other uses as well.

Steel mill.

Finished steel beams.

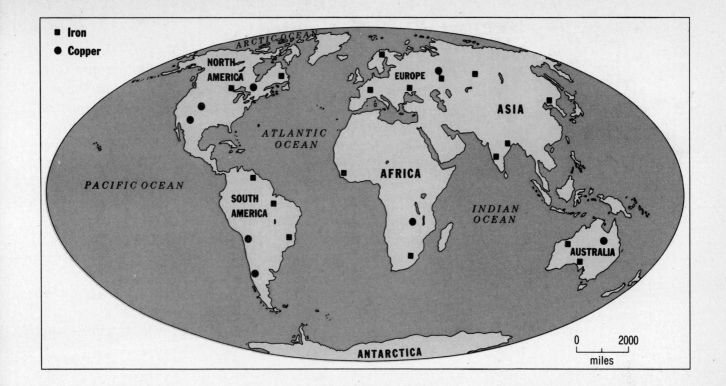

Aluminum is a very light but strong metal. It comes from an ore called bauxite. Aluminum is used to make pots and pans, soft drink cans, bicycle wheels, auto parts, and other things.

Silver and gold are used to make jewelry. These minerals also have many other uses. Silver is used in photography. Gold is used for some dental work. Do you own anything made with silver or gold?

All the minerals we have talked about are nonrenewable. When they are used up, there will be no more of them.

Where Some Metals Are Found

The map above shows where most of the world's iron and copper are found. Use the map to answer these questions.

1. Are there more iron mines or copper mines in the world?

2. Does the United States have any copper?

3. Which continent has the most iron mines?

4. Suppose a country does not have any iron or copper of its own. How do you think it might get these?

Some Resources Are Not Renewable

Problems

Today we are using huge amounts of some nonrenewable resources. We may soon run out of them. We are in danger of ruining some of our renewable resources, too. We are also **polluting** the planet we live on. Let's take a look at some of these problems.

Polluting the Air and Water

Coal and oil are wonderful sources of energy. But when they burn, they add chemicals to the air. Some of the chemicals are harmful to living things and can cause illness and death.

Sometimes the chemicals mix with other things in the air and make **smog.** Smog hangs over cities in a thick dark cloud. It can cause your eyes to water and can make breathing difficult.

Smoke coming out of factory smokestacks may contain harmful chemicals.

Sometimes chemicals in the air mix with rainwater. The water turns the chemicals into **acids.** Acid rain harms the plants it falls on. If it falls on or runs into streams, rivers, or lakes, it can kill fish. Acid rain can be strong enough to dissolve rock.

Water can be polluted in another way. Many factories use tons of water every day. Then, they may dump the used water into rivers and lakes. This water may contain harmful chemicals that can kill plants and fish. Birds and other animals that eat the plants and fish may die also.

We, too, can get sick from eating things that live in polluted water. And we can get sick if we swim in it. We cannot drink polluted water or use it for watering crops.

Oil Spills

Much of the world's oil lies under water. Wells are sunk down from oil-drilling platforms to where the oil is. Sometimes these wells leak, and then the oil spills out, killing fish and other sea life.

Spills are also caused by huge ships, called tankers, that carry oil around the world. Sometimes these tankers leak or even break apart. Then tons of oil spill out into the ocean. The oil kills sea life. It may also wash up onto beaches. Sea birds get coated with the oil. They cannot fly. They may not be able to breathe. Many die.

Mining and Forestry Problems

You read earlier about strip and open pit mines. They are the cheapest and fastest way to get at minerals buried in the ground. But strip mining strips away trees and soil. And open pit mining leaves huge ugly holes in the ground.

Cutting down forests causes problems, too. Can you guess what some of the problems are?

Trees soak up water. When they are gone, rainwater washes away the soil. Wind can blow it away, too.

Trees give off water vapor. When forests are cut down, the climate of a place can change. There may be less rain.

Also, where there is less plant life, there is likely to be less animal life.

These shorebirds became coated with oil from an oil spill that washed ashore. The people are trying to save the birds by cleaning off the oil.

Dealing with the Problems

Many people are working to save our resources. Here are some of the things they are doing.

Pollution Controls

Governments have made laws to control air pollution. Automobiles can release only certain amounts of harmful chemicals into the air. The same is true of factories.

Laws have also been made to control water pollution. Factories are not allowed to dump certain wastes into rivers and lakes. They must remove harmful chemicals from water before they dump it.

Many polluted rivers and lakes are being cleaned up. But it will take years to make them safe again.

Using New Sources of Energy

People are using other sources of energy besides coal and oil. Windmills are being used to make electricity. Some people are trapping heat from the sun with solar panels. You may have seen these panels on some roofs where you live. The energy they collect can help heat a building or make hot water.

Saving and Recycling Resources

People are trying to cut down on the amounts of coal, oil, and other resources they use. They shut off unneeded lights to cut down on the electricity they use. That saves coal and oil, because these resources are burned to produce electricity.

Aluminum cans, plastic and glass bottles, and newspapers can all be easily recycled.

Driving to school or work in carpools is another way to help save oil.

Do you turn in aluminum cans and glass jars and bottles to recycling centers? The metal and glass can be melted down and used again.

Newspapers can be recycled. Some community groups recycle newspapers to raise money.

Old cars and other machines made of metal are also recycled. The metal is melted down and new things are made with it.

Replacing Soil and Trees

Some mining companies now take steps to repair the places they have mined. They fill in open pits. They replace the soil and plant new grass and trees.

Some logging companies also plant new trees after they have cut down part of a forest.

These are some of the things that people are doing to help save our resources.

Can you think of anything you can do to help?

Does your community have a recycling center like this one? If so, what does it collect for recycling?

Summary

1. Scientists believe that oil was formed from dead sea life. We get heating oil, motor oil, gasoline, plastic, and other products from crude oil.
2. Scientists believe coal was formed from layers of dead plants. Coal is used to produce steel and electricity.
3. Metals such as iron and copper are minerals that come from rocks called ores.
4. Coal, oil, and other mineral resources are non-renewable. That is, they cannot be replaced.
5. Some resource problems we face are pollution, oil spills, and the loss of forests and soil.
6. To help solve the problems, we are:
   - limiting the amounts of harmful chemicals that automobiles and factories release into the air
   - putting controls on the dumping of waste water
   - using windmills to produce electricity and solar panels to produce heat
   - shutting off unneeded lights
   - carpooling
   - recycling metal, glass, and paper products
   - replacing and replanting soil in some mining areas
   - replanting some forests after trees are cut down.

Questions to Discuss

1. What are some nonrenewable resources that you use every day? How do you use them?
2. Suppose the world suddenly ran out of oil. How would that affect your life?
3. How can you help save our natural resources?

Special Projects

Form teams. Try to find the answers to the questions below. Report your answers to the class.

1. What kind of air and water pollution problems do you have in your area?
2. Do you live near a recycling center? If so, what does it collect and what happens to the things it collects?

Reading a Pie Graph

A pie graph is useful for showing how a whole thing is divided into parts. For example, the pie graph below shows how much of Earth's surface is water and how much is land.

You can tell which there is more of by the size of each part of the graph. Which is there more of, land or water?

This graph shows that only one-third of Earth's surface is land. All the rest is water.

The pie graph at the bottom of the page shows how the world's oil reserves are divided. Reserve oil is oil that is still in the ground.

Look at the graph. Read the names of the different parts of the world that are listed on the graph. Then answer these questions:

1. Which part of the world has the most oil reserves?
2. Which part of the world has the least oil reserves?
3. Does the Middle East have more or less oil than all the rest of the world?

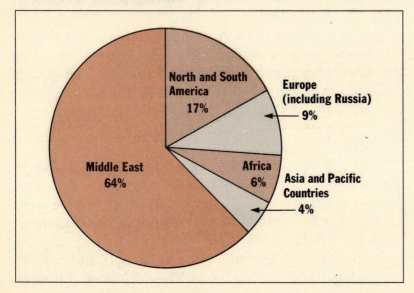

World Oil Reserves

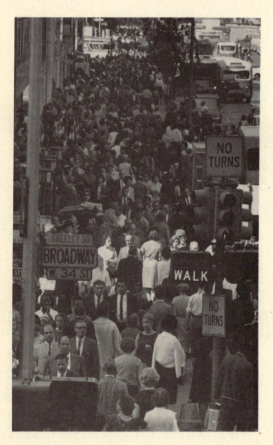

There are now more than 5 billion (5,000,000,000) people living on Earth. To get an idea of how many people that is, think of this: If you were to count one person each second, it would take you about 150 years to count them all.

Early History

Gatherers and Hunters

Earth did not always have so many people. Back 10,000 years ago, its **population** was only about 10 million (10,000,000). Population means the number of people that live in a place.

In those times, people lived in small communities. Most of them were gatherers. To live, they gathered wild seeds, berries, nuts, and other plant food. And they also hunted animals.

Because of the limited amount of food in an area, not too many people could live there. When there were no more plants to pick or animals to kill, the people had to move to other places.

Discoveries

One of the things that greatly changed human life on Earth was the discovery of how to control fire. This helped people stay warm in cold places and protect themselves from wild animals. And it allowed them to cook their food.

People also discovered how to make pots and baskets for cooking and storing foods. They discovered how to make boats for travel on water. They discovered how to make better tools and hunting weapons.

All these improvements led to small increases in the population.

Farmers, Herders, and Craftworkers

In time, some people discovered how to grow plants. They became farmers and raised corn, wheat, rice, and barley.

People also learned to raise sheep, goats, and cattle. They became herders.

In time, people were able to produce more food by farming and herding than they could by hunting and gathering. As the food supply increased, so did the population.

At first, each community raised only enough food for itself. And the community made whatever it needed. But later, communities began to trade things. A community with extra wheat might trade some of it for a goat.

When farmers and herders got better at raising crops and animals, there was less need for everyone to be doing these things. Some people then became craftsworkers. They spent their time making tools, pottery, clothing, baskets, and other useful things.

A craftsworker could trade what he or she had made for food or for something that someone else had made. Later, money was invented. Then people could buy and sell things.

Big changes were also brought about when the wheel was invented. The wheel made it possible to move more things from one place to another.

Cave drawing of a deer hunt.

The Growth of Towns and Cities

Villages of farmers and craftsworkers appeared at different places around the world. After a long time, villages grew into towns and cities. Here are just a few of the reasons some villages grew.

- They had good farmland that could support larger populations.
- They were near sources of water that could be used to water crops in dry seasons.
- They were near resources that could be used to build or make things.
- They were next to waterways and had places for boats to load and unload goods.

Some places became cities because strong rulers built forts there. People came to live in the cities because they felt safer and could earn a living there. Later, cities offered other attractions as well, such as temples, theaters, and sports arenas.

People started building cities about 6,000 years ago. By that time, Earth's population had grown to about 85 million (85,000,000).

The ancient city of Babylon was founded on very fertile land between two rivers.

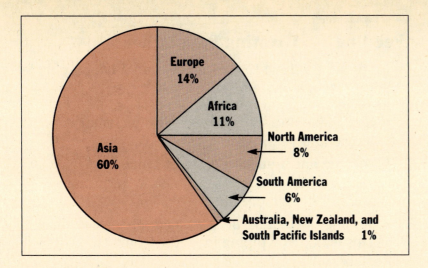

Recent Changes

The biggest growth in Earth's population has come in recent times. The growth came because people began to understand the importance of **sanitation**. Sanitation means safely getting rid of garbage and human wastes. Sanitation helped prevent disease, which saved lives. New medicines also helped save lives. By 1925 the population reached 2 billion (2,000,000,000).

Then scientists began to find ways to stop the spread of terrible diseases. The shots you took as a child to keep you from getting smallpox and other killer diseases are one example of this. Such diseases used to kill millions of people.

Shots, other improvements in health care, and larger food supplies kept more people alive. By 1975 the population doubled, to 4 billion (4,000,000,000).

Since then, the number has grown by over a billion more.

The pie graph above compares the size of each continent's population as of 1985. Except for some scientists, no one lives on Antartica, so it is not included on the graph.

Study the pie graph. Then answer these questions:

1. Which continent has the largest number of people?
2. What percent of the world's population lives there?
3. Do Asians make up more than or less than half of the world's population?
4. What percent of the world's population lives in North America?

Feeding the Growing Population

It takes a lot of food to feed more than 5 billion people. Where is it all coming from?

- Giant machines help farmers produce more than they could years ago.
- Science has found ways to get more food from corn, wheat, and rice plants. Some farmlands now produce more food.
- Some deserts have been turned into farmlands. This is done by piping in water from other places.
- Science has found ways to raise bigger animals that produce more meat.

Sometimes, there are famines in parts of the world. A famine is a severe food shortage. It can happen when the country gets much less rain than usual. It can happen when disease, floods, or war destroy crops. And it can happen when people do not have enough money to buy food.

Some people are worried. They say that if the population keeps growing as fast as it is growing now, there will not be enough food for everyone.

Others say that producing enough food is not the real problem. They believe that each country's farmlands could produce enough food to meet that country's needs. But too often, they say, farmlands are not used to raise crops that are needed. Instead they are used to raise animals and crops that can be sold for high prices, often to other countries.

A windmill helps pump water to a vegetable garden in Thailand.

Summary

1. Thousands of years ago, people were gatherers and hunters of food. Earth's population stayed small—about 10 million. As people found better ways to grow and raise food, the population began to grow.

2. People become farmers, herders, and craftsworkers. They started to trade and to set up villages. Some villages grew into cities. About 6,000 years ago, Earth's population reached 85 million.

3. In more recent times, improved sanitation and new medicines led to people's living longer. By 1925 Earth's population had reached 2 billion.

4. In the next 50 years, Earth's population doubled to 4 billion. It has now reached more than 5 billion and is still growing. The main reasons for the growth are improvements in health care and increases in the food supply.

5. Some people worry that there will not be enough food to feed an ever-growing population. Others say that the problem is in how some farmlands are used.

Questions to Discuss

1. How does the way you and your family get food differ from the way gatherers and hunters got theirs?

2. Why do you think so many people choose to live in cities today?

3. What part has science and medicine played in helping Earth's population more than double since 1925?

Special Projects

1. Find out the population of your town or city. Is the population increasing or decreasing? Try to find the reason for any changes.

2. Find out more about the gatherers and hunters who lived long ago or about Earth's early cities. Report to the class.

How We Live

People everywhere have the same basic needs. They need food, clothing, and shelter. They need love, friendship, and a sense of belonging.

But different groups of people meet their needs in different ways. Each group has its own **culture.** Culture is the way a group of people thinks and acts.

A culture group may include all the people who live in a country. Or it may be a small group that chooses to live a certain way.

Here are some things that may differ from one culture to another. There are others as well, such as clothing, music, and art.

Food

Many Americans like fried, mashed, or baked potatoes with their main meal. That is part of the American culture.

Most Asians prefer rice. Italians often prefer spaghetti or similar foods made from grain. That is part of their culture.

The ways people prepare food may also be very different. Most Americans cook the fish they eat. But most Japanese eat both raw and cooked fish.

Today, Americans eat foods from many of the world's cultures. Do you eat pizza, bagels, or tacos? They were brought to the United States by people who came here from other countries.

What foods are special to the culture you come from?

Jai Alai has become part of the American culture as more and more Americans play and watch it.

Things to Find Out

1. What culture groups are
2. Some ways in which cultures are different
3. Why there are so many different cultures in the United States

Sports and Games

Sports of some kind are played in most cultures. Many were started as a way to learn skills for hunting and war. For example, young children might play with wooden spears. This helped develop the skills they would need for hunting and fighting when they grew up.

Many cultures have games that call for the use of a bat and ball. Others have games that call for putting a ball through a hoop. Out of these games came the American sports of baseball and basketball.

Soccer was started in England. It became very popular in Europe and then spread to Latin America. Latin America includes Mexico and all the countries south of it. Now soccer is being played by many Americans.

Family Life

In some cultures, only parents and their children live together. The parents provide for their children. The children may also help out as they grow older.

In other cultures, parents and their children may live together with other relatives. They may live with grandparents, aunts, uncles, and cousins. They may all live under the same roof or close by to each other.

In this larger family, all able grown-ups in the family help meet the family's needs. The older children may help on a family farm or in a family business. They may care for younger children and for family members who are sick or in need of help.

How do you think living close to many relatives differs from living with only parents, brothers, and sisters?

Related families gather for a reunion.

Language

Language is an important part of culture. Through it, people share their stories, ideas, and feelings. With language, they learn from one another.

There are about 3,000 different languages in the world. Some are spoken by only a few hundred people. Others are spoken by millions.

Which language do you think is spoken by more people than any other?

More people speak Mandarin, a form of Chinese, than any other language. The second most widely spoken language is English.

Languages Spread and Change

Most of today's languages started from a few main languages spoken thousands of years ago. As people spread out over Earth, they took their languages with them.

Over time, the sounds of some words changed. The meanings of some words also changed. Some words dropped out of the language because they were no longer used. New words were added as people discovered and did new things.

Other changes came when one country would take over another. This is how English started.

At different times, different European countries took over parts of England. Each time, the people living there had to learn the language of their new rulers. England's language became a mixture of French, German, and other European languages.

English was first brought to America by the people who came here from England in the 1600s. Today, American English has added many words from the languages of different culture groups that live here. For example, we get *tornado* from Spanish. *Pizza* comes from Italian. And *chow mein* is from Chinese.

Religion

Many people belong to a religion. In North America, Christianity, Judaism, and Islam have the largest number of followers. There are also many followers of Hinduism, Buddhism, and Confucianism.

Though religions are different, they share some things in common.

Most religions have beliefs about how the world and its people were created. Some, but not all, believe in a god or gods who greatly affect life on Earth.

Most religions teach how people should act and how they should treat others. They usually promise everlasting peace and happiness for those who follow the teachings of the religion.

The teachings of most religions are set down in special writings. Christians have the Bible. Jews follow the Torah and the Talmud. Others follow the Koran or the Vedas.

These writings often tell more than just the beliefs of the religion. They also tell about the history of the religion and about the lives of its leaders.

Each religion has its own way of praying. This may include singing, dancing, lighting candles, or leaving food or other gifts. Such things as birth, coming of age, marriage, and death are also celebrated in special ways.

How Religions Spread

Most of the world's popular religions were started by leaders with strong beliefs. While they were alive, these leaders traveled and taught. Later, many of their followers went out to spread the teachings.

That is one way some religions grew and spread. Another way was by people taking their religion with them when they moved to other lands.

A Buddhist temple.

People on the Move

People from many different cultures live in the United States. That is because people have **migrated** to America from all over the world. To migrate is to move from one place to another.

Migration is nothing new. Hunters and gatherers migrated to North America from Asia many thousands of years ago. They were looking for food.

About 500 years ago, people from Europe started migrating to North and South America. Many of them were looking for riches. Some were looking for freedom. Many wanted a chance to own land or to earn a better living.

Some people were forced to migrate. About 20 million people came to North and South America from Africa. They were brought here as slaves.

Migration Is Still Going On

Today, there are still large migrations of people. Recent wars have forced millions of people to leave their homes in Southeast Asia, Central America, and the Middle East. Many of these people have migrated to the United States. Many people also have come here from poor countries in order to find work.

All these people have brought with them their languages, religions, and other parts of their cultures.

Many people migrate within their own countries. They migrate from farms to cities. They migrate from one city to another in search of work. And many people migrate from colder climates to warmer climates.

Have you migrated recently? Do you know anyone who has?

The Dust Bowl of the 1930s forced many American families to migrate from the Midwest.

Summary

1. Culture is the way a group of people thinks and acts. Some of the things that may differ from one culture to another are: art, clothing, family life, games and sports, food, language, and religion.

2. Many foods from other countries have become part of the American diet.

3. Most cultures have sports and games. Many of them started as ways to develop special skills.

4. In some cultures, large groups of relatives live together or close by each other. They help one another.

5. Most languages come from a few main languages that changed as people spread out over Earth.

6. There are a number of different religions. They have different teachings, beliefs, ways to pray, and ways to mark events like births and marriages.

7. Millions of people have migrated to the United States. Each new group adds something new to American culture.

Questions to Discuss

1. What are some of the foods Americans eat that come from other cultures?

2. How would life be different if everyone living in the United States came from the same culture?

3. Tell why you agree or disagree with this statement: The mix of cultures in America makes life more interesting and enjoyable.

Special Projects

1. Prepare a report about your family. Add pictures and maps. Write about the culture you come from. What are some of its beliefs, foods, games, and special events?

2. Report on your family's migrations. Where were you born? Where did your parents come from? Where did your grandparents come from?

12

MAKING, BUYING, AND SELLING THINGS

Do you own a bike, watch, or radio? Each of these things is made in a factory. A factory is a building where products are made with the help of machines.

Industry

The First U.S. Factories

In 1845 Americans began building factories in the northeastern United States, where there are many rivers and waterfalls. The moving water was used to turn large waterwheels. The waterwheels then drove the moving parts of machines.

The Northeast also had two big **port** cities, Boston and New York. **Raw materials** could be brought in by ship and finished goods shipped out.

Raw materials are the things that go into making a product. For example, leather, rubber, and glue are raw materials for making shoes.

Steel and Auto Industries

Later in the 1800s, America's steel industry grew up near the Great Lakes. An industry is a group of companies that make similar products or that offer similar services.

The steel industry started in the Great Lakes region for three main reasons:

- Large amounts of iron ore were found in Minnesota and Michigan. Iron is melted with other metals to make steel.

Pennsylvania steel furnaces, 1905.

Geography

Things to Find Out

1. How and where factories started
2. Why countries trade with one another
3. Why there are rich and poor countries

- The iron ore could be shipped cheaply by boat on the Great Lakes.
- Large amounts of coal were found in the Appalachian mountain states. Coal was needed to produce the heat that melts the iron and other metals.

Steel mills were soon making steel in Chicago, Cleveland, Pittsburgh, and other nearby cities within reach of the iron mines and coal fields.

Later, a new industry began in the Great Lakes area. Steel from nearby mills was used to manufacture, or make, cars and trucks.

Industries Change

In recent times, many companies that used steel began buying it from other countries, where it was cheaper. Many steel mills and coal mines closed in the United States and thousands of workers lost their jobs.

At the same time, new centers of industry grew in other parts of the country. Big shipping ports and large amounts of oil and natural gas attracted businesses to California and Texas. Lower pay for workers and other lower costs attracted many businesses to the South.

Another big change was the growth of service industries. Service is something that is done for someone. Cooks, nurses, sales clerks, and firefighters all provide services. In the United States, there are now more service workers than workers who produce goods.

Trading Between Countries

Most of the world's nonfood products are made in only a small number of countries. Some of the biggest producers are the United States, Japan, Canada, and the countries of western Europe. How do people in other countries get the things they need or want?

Countries trade with one another. Or rather, business people in one country trade with business people in other countries.

Some countries have a lot of oil, copper, or other resources. But they may not have enough money to build factories of their own. Or they may be just beginning to manufacture their own products.

These countries **export** their resources to countries that will buy them. And they import the things they want from countries that make them.

To *export* goods is to *sell* them to other countries. To *import* goods is to *buy* them from other countries.

Three Examples

Nigeria is a country that has a lot of oil. But it does not have many factories. Nigeria exports oil and imports manufactured goods.

Japan has few resources. But it has a large highly trained population and a good deal of money. Japan imports oil and raw materials from other countries. It turns raw materials into cars, computers, radios, TV sets, and other goods.

Some of these products stay in Japan and are bought there. The rest are exported to other countries.

The United States imports cars, clothing, and other products even though it also makes these things. The main reason is that these things often can be made more cheaply in other countries. Companies in many other countries have lower costs than companies in the United States. Also, these goods may sometimes be better made in other countries.

Take a look at the clothing you are wearing. Your shoes may come from Brazil. Your shirt or blouse may come from Taiwan or Hong Kong. Your watch may come from Japan. Check the labels on the things you own to see where your clothing and other things come from.

Food

Countries export foods they can sell in other countries. They import foods they do not grow enough of at home.

Some countries grow food mainly for export instead of for meeting their people's food needs. That is, they grow crops such as coffee or bananas that will bring high prices in other countries.

Some foods are imported because they are cheaper in other countries. In many cases, though, imported foods cost more.

What foods have you eaten that you know came from other countries?

Making, Buying, and Selling Things

Rich Countries and Poor Countries

The countries of the world have not all developed, or built up, their industries at the same speed. The United States, Japan, Canada, and the countries of western Europe have developed much faster than most other countries. They are the richer countries of the world.

A few countries are developing quickly. But many countries have few industries or resources. And some of them are very poor.

The Developed Countries

Most of the developed countries began building up their industries more than a hundred years ago. They had a head start on the other countries.

Industry brings wealth or money to a country. Because of their industries, developed countries have more jobs for their people. When people have jobs, they have money to spend.

If the people earn more than they need for food, clothing, and shelter, then they can buy other things. They can buy radios, TV sets, and other products. That, in turn, may lead to the building of more factories to make all the things people want to buy.

When people have jobs they have money to spend.

96

Developing Countries

One reason some countries have few industries is that they were once ruled by strong countries in Europe. The ruling countries removed much of the resources and wealth of countries they ruled. Later, when the countries became free, they lacked money and skilled workers to build up their own industries.

Some of the developing countries have resources they can sell. The poorer ones sell their resources to the developed countries. Most of the money they earn goes for food, farm machinery, and medicine. Other developing countries can also buy cars, radios, TV sets, and other products people like to have.

Some developing countries have gained wealth because they have oil and can sell it to developed countries.

Farming in Developing Countries

Some developing countries such as Chad have few, if any, resources to sell. They may have few, if any, industries. Often there aren't many jobs. People live mainly from the food they can grow themselves.

Most of the farmers in these countries are too poor to buy the land and machinery needed to grow more food. They can only produce enough for their own families. If there is a famine, the people often go hungry.

In some of the countries that grow crops for export, such as Guatemala, a few people or companies own most of the farmland. Farm workers earn very little and have little or no land to grow their own food.

One developing country that has made improvements in farming is Zimbabwe. It is now better able to feed people without having to import food. This leaves more money to develop industries.

Helping the Developing Countries

Developed countries have helped developing countries. They've given or loaned money. They've sent food in times of famine.

Many teachers, doctors, nurses, and other trained workers go to developing countries. They've been able to help many people improve their lives. But sometimes ideas that come from one region or one culture don't work well in another. Then people must keep looking for new ways that work.

Will the poor countries ever catch up with the rich countries, or even come close? Only time will tell.

The woman on the left is an English teacher visiting Botswana, Africa, from the United States. The woman on the right is showing her a traditional method of sifting flour.

Geography

Summary

1. In modern factories, workers turn out products by machine instead of by hand.
2. The first factories in the United States were in the Northeast. The Northeast had two big ports and the water power needed to run machines.
3. America's steel industry began near the Great Lakes, close to large amounts of iron and coal.
4. The auto industry started and grew in Detroit, Michigan, close to a ready supply of steel.
5. Countries trade with one another. They export, or sell, certain goods. And they import, or buy, certain goods.
6. Only a small number of the world's countries have developed large industries. Others are just beginning to develop their industries. Most of the developing countries are poor.

Questions to Discuss

1. What are some of the reasons industries start where they do?
2. Why might some countries be richer than others?
3. Do you think the rich, developed countries of the world should help the others? Why or why not?

Special Projects

1. Find out what kind of factories are in your town, city, or state. What products do they make? Are they part of an industry that is growing, staying about the same size, or becoming smaller?
2. Find out which countries these foods come from:
   - bananas
   - black pepper
   - coconuts
   - cocoa
   - coffee
   - jalapeño peppers
   - olives
   - vanilla beans

13

MOVING GOODS, PEOPLE, AND IDEAS

Transportation

Think back to the days of the early hunters and gatherers. At that time, people had only one way to get themselves and their belongings from place to place. They walked wherever they were going. They carried their belongings on their heads or backs.

A giant step forward in moving people and goods came with the invention of the wheel. Once people had wheels, they could build carts and wagons.

Animals were also used to help people **transport** themselves and their belongings. To transport means to carry. Animals pulling carts and wagons could transport large heavy loads over long distances.

The Growth of Road Systems

When people walked back and forth between villages, they made paths and trails. When they started using carts and wagons, they widened the paths and trails into roadways. As villages became towns and towns became cities, roadways were paved.

In the poorer countries of the world, many villages are stilled connected only by paths, trails, or dirt roads. There, most of the people still travel by foot or on animals. They still use carts and wagons to carry their goods.

The richer countries of the world are crisscrossed by paved roads. In the United States, people can now drive on 42,500 miles of **interstate highways.** These highways connect the country's major cities and towns.

Things to Find Out

1. How footpaths and trails became roads and highways
2. How inventions changed the way people travel, move goods, and send messages

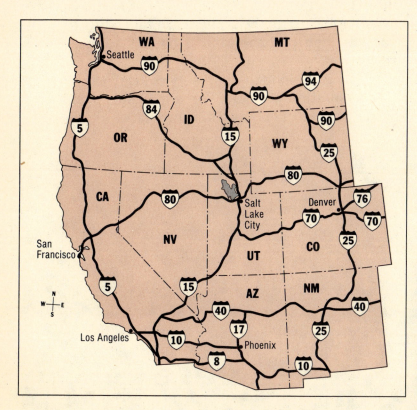

Each state also has many other streets, roads, and highways.

The map above shows part of the U.S. interstate highway system. Each highway has a number. Use the map to answer the first two questions below:

1. Which highway will take you all the way from Los Angeles, California, to Seattle, Washington?

2. Which highway will take you from Los Angeles to Salt Lake City, Utah?

3. Which interstate highway do you live closest to?

Moving Goods, People, and Ideas

Trucks

Trucks are the fastest growing form of transportation in the United States. They carry loads that weigh many thousands of pounds. They can go anywhere there are roads for them to travel on.

Many trucks have cooling systems. This allows them to carry foods that need to be kept cold.

One kind of truck has a separate tractor and trailer. The tractor does the pulling. The trailer carries the load. A driver can deliver a trailer and leave it to be unloaded. Then he or she can pick up another trailer.

Sometimes the trailers are put on trains for long trips. A train can carry dozens of loaded trailers. At the end of the trip, the trailers are taken off the train. Tractors then pull the loaded trailers to where they are going.

Trucks give door-to-door service. But they add to the air pollution problem. For some kinds of shipping, they are not as cheap as trains or boats.

Geography

Railroads

The first railroads were built well over 100 years ago, before cars and trucks were invented. They gave people a way to travel more safely and quickly. They gave companies a way of sending heavy loads over mountains that wagons couldn't cross. A trip that once took weeks by wagon took only days by train.

Many of America's towns grew up beside railroad tracks. Big cities grew where trains from different places all came together at a port.

Not many Americans take long train trips anymore. They drive cars or take airplanes instead. But in and around some of America's big cities, millions of people ride trains to work and school. That helps save oil and cuts down on air pollution. Trains also carry millions of pounds of food, resources, raw materials, and finished products every day.

Trains are cheaper than trucks for sending large shipments over long distances. But they can only go where there are tracks.

Many people take trains to and from work or school. How can this cut down on air pollution?

The building of the Panama Canal, 1913.

Water Transportation

People learned long ago that they could travel and transport goods over water. At first, they used rafts and small boats. Later, they built bigger boats and ships that could cross oceans.

In the 1700s, a sailing trip across the Atlantic Ocean took about 2½ months. By 1900 ships with steam engines took only seven days. Today, some ships can make the trip in five days.

Inland Waterways

Much of the world's goods are carried by boat or barge on inland waterways. A barge is a large flat-bottomed boat.

One of the world's longest inland waterways is the Mississippi River. Barges loaded with coal, corn, wheat, and other products travel on the Mississippi.

Near the mouth of the river, at the port of New Orleans, **cargo** is moved from the barges onto ocean-going ships. Then it is shipped around the world.

Canals Help Shipping

Canals are often dug to connect two or more bodies of water. In Europe, they connect many of the large rivers. This makes it possible for shippers to send goods hundreds of miles by inland waterways. Canals are also important in England and in China.

One of the most important canals for world shipping is the Panama Canal. It connects the Atlantic and Pacific Oceans. Ships pass through the canal instead of going all the way around South America. This saves 8,000 miles on a trip from Atlantic to Pacific ports.

Transporting goods over water is usually the cheapest way to move them long distances. But it is also the slowest. And cargo can only be sent where ships and boats can go.

Air Travel

Air travel is less than 100 years old. The early planes were tiny and flew only short distances. But later, planes got bigger, faster, and safer.

In the 1950s, planes began to use jet engines. Most of today's jetliners fly at speeds between 500 and 600 miles an hour. Some jetliners fly at 1,500 miles an hour.

Passenger planes carry people and mail. They may also carry small amounts of cargo. Cargo planes carry only cargo.

The fastest way to ship things is by plane. But it is also the most expensive way. And shipments can only be sent to where there are airports. From there, they travel by truck to where they are going.

Pipelines and Cable Links

Much of what we need does not come to us by truck, train, ship, or plane. For example, how does water get to your house?

Most homes, factories, and businesses get their water through pipelines. Other pipelines carry wastes away from those places.

Pipelines also carry oil and natural gas. The Alaska Pipeline is 800 miles long. It carries oil from Prudhoe Bay to the port of Valdez.

Cables are another kind of carrier. Some cables carry electrical power from place to place. Other cables carry telephone messages. TV programs are also sent out over cables.

Communication

Have you talked on the telephone, watched TV, or listened to the radio lately? All of these allow the sending of messages that can be received at almost the same moment they are sent.

Long ago, messages were sent by drums. The drummer used a code. Each set of drumbeats meant something. Drums are still used in some places to send messages back and forth.

Telegraph

The beginning of a new age in sending messages came in 1844. That's when telegraph machines were first used. Like the drum, a telegraph machine sends messages in code. But the messages go out over wires.

Telephone

The trouble with the telegraph was that it could only send coded messages, not the sound of someone speaking. In 1876 Alexander Graham Bell invented the telephone. Today, we can call and talk to people in almost any country in the world.

Alexander Graham Bell with an early version of his telephone.

Radio

Telephones, too, had a problem. They had to be hooked up to each other with telephone lines.

In 1921 Guglielmo Marconi found a way of sending telegraph signals without using wires. This led to the invention of the radio. Today, even in places that do not have telephones, people can get messages by radio.

Television

The first television show was in 1936. In the 1950s, television became popular. Today, it gives us a chance to see the world without leaving our homes.

We see sports events from all over the world. We see floods, storms, and even war. Often, we see these things as they are happening.

Television also helps us learn about other people's cultures—about their foods, clothing, music, and ways of life. At the same time, people in other countries are learning about us.

Computers

Another way to send and receive messages quickly is with computers. The amount of information that travels back and forth on computers is growing every day. New ways are continually being found to put these machines to work.

Used widely, all these forms of communication can help the people of the world become neighbors rather than strangers.

Computers are changing the ways in which we communicate with each other.

Summary

1. In poor countries people still travel on foot and move goods with animals, carts, and wagons.

2. The richer countries of the world have many good roads. In the United States, the interstate highway system connects most big cities and towns.

3. Trucks give door-to-door service but add to pollution problems. Truck transport is usually more costly than rail or water transport.

4. Train transport is often cheaper than truck, but trains can only go where there are tracks.

5. Water transport is the cheapest but the slowest way to move goods. It is limited to where ships can go.

6. Air travel is the fastest but also the most expensive way to move goods. It is limited to where there are airports.

7. Pipelines carry such things as water, oil, natural gas, and wastes. Cables carry electricity, telephone messages, and TV programs.

8. Many inventions have made it possible to receive messages at almost the same time they are sent.

Questions to Discuss

1. How would your life be different if cars, trucks, and buses had never been invented?

2. How would your life be different if the radio, television, and telephone had never been invented?

3. What new ways do you think people might find for traveling and for sending goods and messages?

Special Projects

1. Find out all you can about the transportation in your area. Is there an airport, train station, or bus station nearby? How do people who live near you travel? How do companies near you ship goods?

2. Get maps of roads and bus or train lines in your area. Plan how you would get from one place to another.

ATLAS

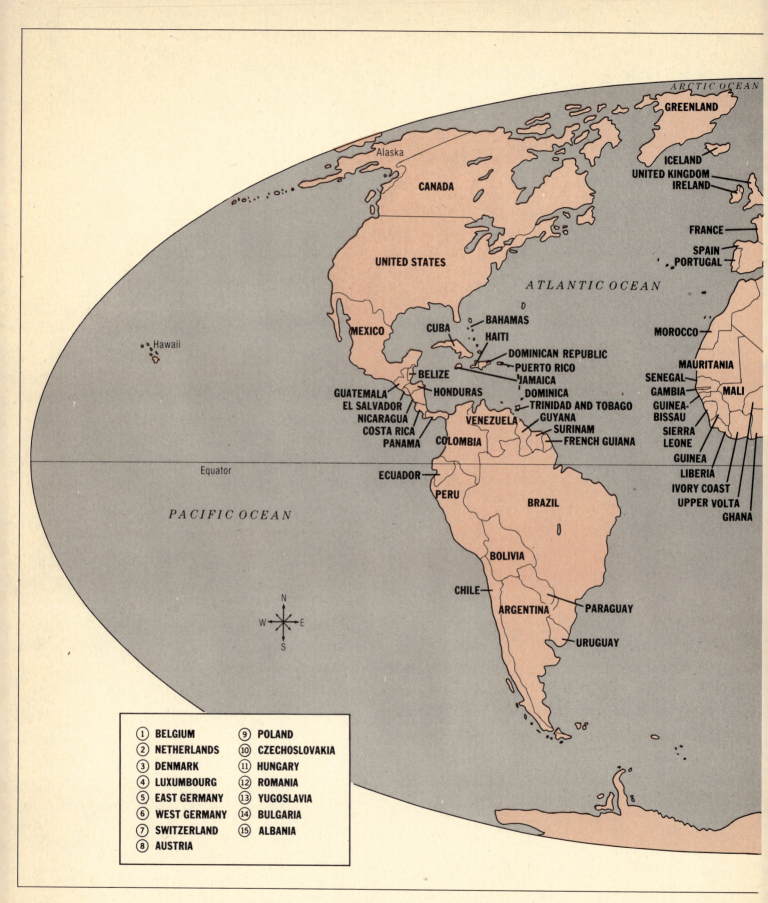

GREENLAND

Alaska

ICELAND
UNITED KINGDOM
IRELAND

CANADA

FRANCE

SPAIN
PORTUGAL

UNITED STATES

ATLANTIC OCEAN

Hawaii

BAHAMAS

MOROCCO

MEXICO
CUBA
HAITI

DOMINICAN REPUBLIC
PUERTO RICO

MAURITANIA

SENEGAL
GAMBIA

MALI

BELIZE
JAMAICA
DOMINICA

GUINEA-
BISSAU

GUATEMALA
EL SALVADOR
NICARAGUA
COSTA RICA
PANAMA

HONDURAS

TRINIDAD AND TOBAGO

VENEZUELA

GUYANA
SURINAM
FRENCH GUIANA

SIERRA
LEONE

COLOMBIA

GUINEA

LIBERIA
IVORY COAST
UPPER VOLTA
GHANA

Equator

ECUADOR

PERU

BRAZIL

PACIFIC OCEAN

BOLIVIA

N

CHILE

W   E

ARGENTINA

PARAGUAY

S

URUGUAY

①	BELGIUM	⑨	POLAND
②	NETHERLANDS	⑩	CZECHOSLOVAKIA
③	DENMARK	⑪	HUNGARY
④	LUXUMBOURG	⑫	ROMANIA
⑤	EAST GERMANY	⑬	YUGOSLAVIA
⑥	WEST GERMANY	⑭	BULGARIA
⑦	SWITZERLAND	⑮	ALBANIA
⑧	AUSTRIA		

WORLD POLITICAL MAP

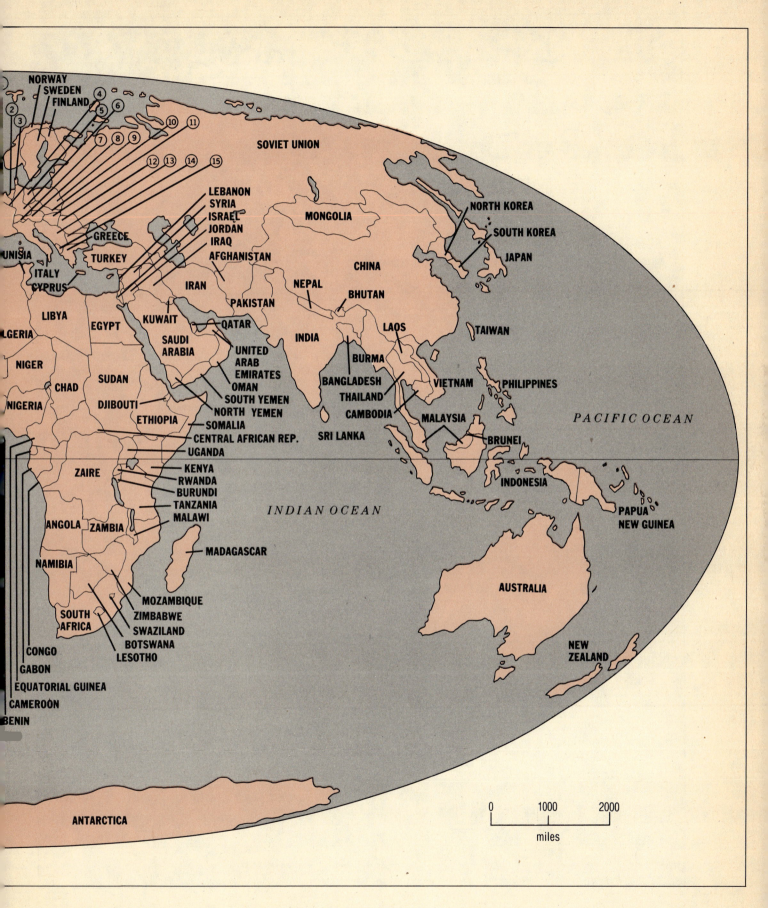

NORWAY
SWEDEN
FINLAND
② ④ ⑥
③ ⑤
⑩ ⑪
⑦ ⑧ ⑨
SOVIET UNION
⑫ ⑬ ⑭ ⑮
MONGOLIA
NORTH KOREA
SOUTH KOREA
JAPAN
LEBANON
SYRIA
ISRAEL
JORDAN
IRAQ
AFGHANISTAN
GREECE
TURKEY
CHINA
TUNISIA
ITALY
CYPRUS
IRAN
NEPAL
BHUTAN
TAIWAN
LIBYA
EGYPT
KUWAIT
PAKISTAN
ALGERIA
SAUDI
ARABIA
QATAR
INDIA
LAOS
NIGER
UNITED
ARAB
EMIRATES
OMAN
BURMA
VIETNAM
PHILIPPINES
CHAD
SUDAN
SOUTH YEMEN
BANGLADESH
THAILAND
NIGERIA
DJIBOUTI
NORTH YEMEN
ETHIOPIA
SOMALIA
CAMBODIA
MALAYSIA
PACIFIC OCEAN
CENTRAL AFRICAN REP.
SRI LANKA
BRUNEI
UGANDA
ZAIRE
KENYA
RWANDA
BURUNDI
INDONESIA
TANZANIA
INDIAN OCEAN
PAPUA
NEW GUINEA
MALAWI
ANGOLA
ZAMBIA
MADAGASCAR
NAMIBIA
AUSTRALIA
MOZAMBIQUE
ZIMBABWE
SOUTH
AFRICA
SWAZILAND
BOTSWANA
LESOTHO
NEW
ZEALAND
CONGO
GABON
EQUATORIAL GUINEA
CAMEROON
BENIN

ANTARCTICA

0   1000   2000
miles

111

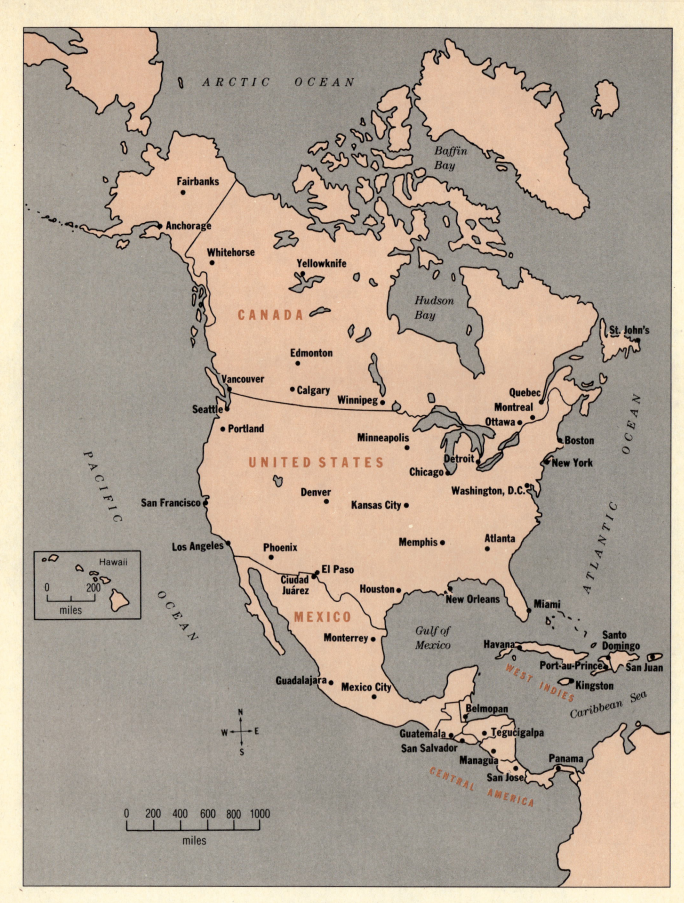

ARCTIC OCEAN

Baffin Bay

Fairbanks

Anchorage

Whitehorse

Yellowknife

Hudson Bay

CANADA

St. John's

Edmonton

Vancouver

Calgary

Winnipeg

Quebec
Montreal
Ottawa

Seattle

Portland

Minneapolis

Boston

Detroit

New York

Chicago

UNITED STATES

Washington, D.C.

PACIFIC

San Francisco

Denver

Kansas City

ATLANTIC

Los Angeles

Phoenix

Memphis

Atlanta

OCEAN

El Paso

Ciudad Juárez

Houston

New Orleans

Miami

Hawaii

0   200

miles

MEXICO

Gulf of Mexico

Havana

Santo Domingo

Port-au-Prince

San Juan

WEST INDIES

Monterrey

Kingston

Caribbean Sea

Guadalajara

Mexico City

N

Belmopan

W   E

Guatemala

Tegucigalpa

S

San Salvador

Managua

Panama

San Jose

CENTRAL AMERICA

0   200   400   600   800   1000

miles

NORTH AMERICAN POLITICAL MAP

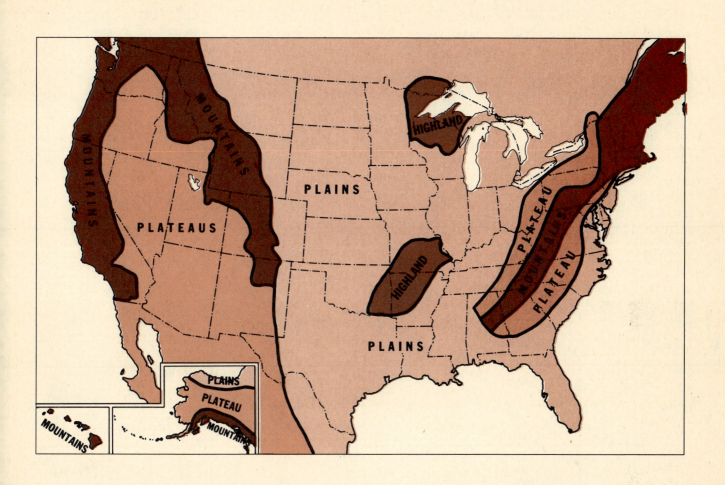

UNITED STATES PHYSICAL MAP

113

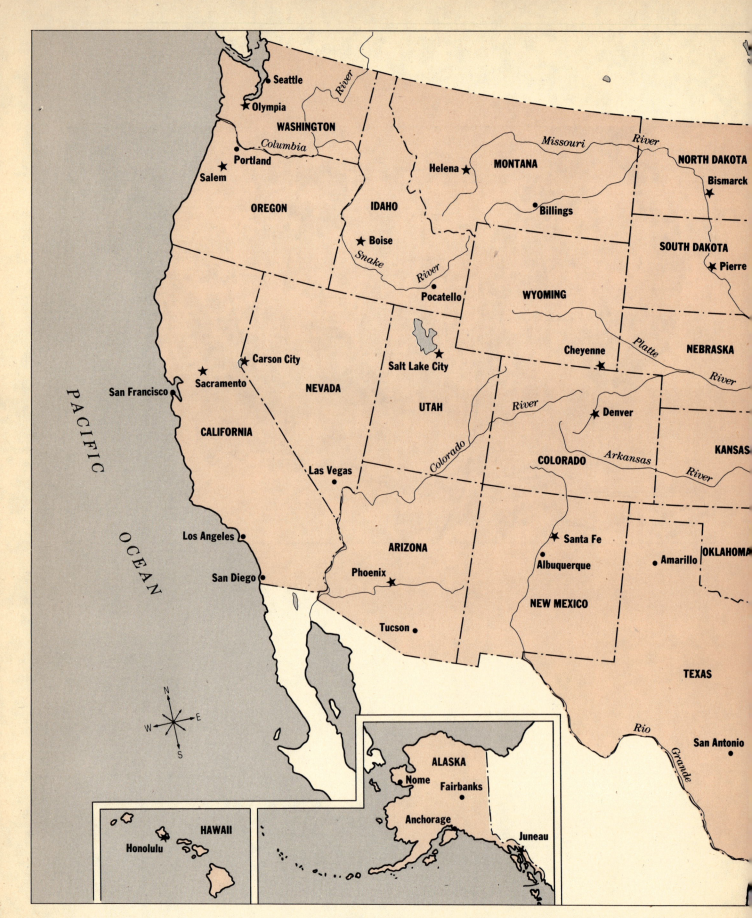

PACIFIC

OCEAN

Seattle

Olympia

WASHINGTON

Columbia

Portland

Salem

OREGON

River

Helena

MONTANA

Missouri

River

NORTH DAKOTA

Bismarck

IDAHO

Boise

Billings

Snake

River

SOUTH DAKOTA

Pierre

Pocatello

WYOMING

Carson City

Salt Lake City

Cheyenne

Platte

NEBRASKA

Sacramento

NEVADA

UTAH

River

Denver

River

San Francisco

CALIFORNIA

Colorado

Arkansas

KANSAS

Las Vegas

COLORADO

River

Los Angeles

Santa Fe

Amarillo

OKLAHOMA

San Diego

ARIZONA

Phoenix

Albuquerque

Tucson

NEW MEXICO

TEXAS

N

W   E

S

Rio

San Antonio

ALASKA

Nome

Fairbanks

Grande

Anchorage

HAWAII

Juneau

Honolulu

114

UNITED STATES POLITICAL MAP

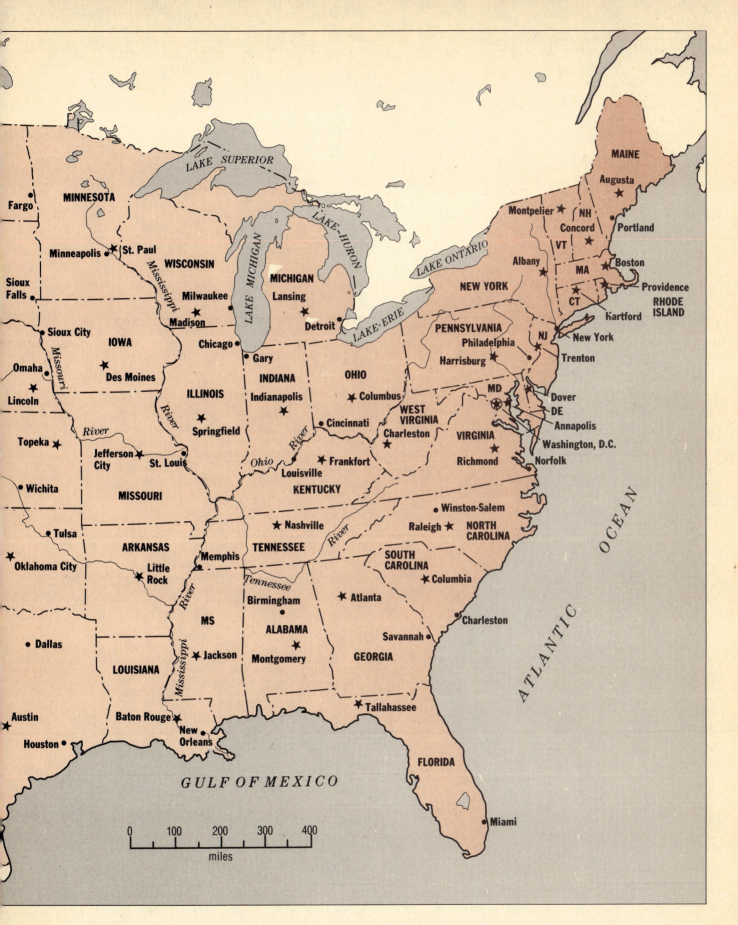

GLOSSARY

a cid a substance that wears away other substances

at mo sphere the layers of air above Earth's surface

bay an inlet of an ocean or other body of water,
usually smaller than a gulf

broad leaf a kind of tree with wide leaves rather
than needle-shaped leaves

ca nal an inland waterway that has been dug by
people rather than by nature

can yon a deep valley with very steep walls, such as
the Grand Canyon

car bon di ox ide a gas that is breathed out by
animals and taken in by plants

car go the goods carried on a ship or plane

cli mate the usual yearly weather of a place

com pass rose an aid to finding which way on a
map is north or to finding any of the
other directions

con ti nent a very large body of land; Earth is divided
into seven continents

core the center of Earth

crude oil oil from under the ground before it is made
into a product, such as gasoline

crust Earth's outer layer

cul ture the ways in which a group of people think
and act

cur rent a large stream of water that flows in an
ocean and that is either colder or warmer
than the water it flows through

del ta islands and sandbars made from sediment
dropped by a river

dune a hill of sand

earth quake the shaking of part of Earth's crust
caused by breaking or slipping rocks
within the crust

e lec tri ci ty a kind of energy

el e va tion the height of the land above sea level

en er gy   the power to do work

e qua tor   the line on a globe halfway between the North and South poles that divides Earth into the Northern and Southern hemispheres

e ros ion   the carrying away of weathered rock

e vap o rate   to turn into tiny droplets that are too small to be seen

ex port   to sell goods to other countries

fault   a deep crack in Earth's crust

fer til iz er   a substance added to soil to provide nutrients

fuel   material that is burned to provide energy

gla cier   a very large moving body of ice and snow

grav i ty   a strong pulling force from inside Earth

gulf   an inlet of an ocean or other large body of water, usually larger than a bay

hem i sphere   half of a ball

hill   a landform that is similar to a mountain but not as high

hu mus   dead plant and animal matter that provides plants with nutrients

hur ri cane   a strong storm that has fast-moving winds and often heavy rain

im port   to buy goods from another country

in ter state   high way   a highway that runs from one state to another

is land   a landform that is surrounded on all sides by water

lake   a body of water surrounded on all sides by land

land form   a feature of Earth's surface, such as a mountain, hill, plateau, or plain

lan guage   the words and sounds used by a group of people to express thoughts and feelings

la va   melted rock from inside the Earth that flows over the land when a volcano erupts

mag ma   the melted rock below Earth's crust

main land   the largest part of a country that is separated from one or more of its parts by water or by land belonging to another country

man tle   the layer of very hot rock between Earth's crust and outer core

mi grate   to move from one place to another

min er al   a usable substance, such as coal, oil, or iron, that is found in Earth's crust

mois ture   wetness

moun tain   a landform that rises very high above sea level and the surrounding land

nee dle leaf   a kind of tree that has leaves shaped like needles

nu tri ent   a substance in soil that gives plants what they need to grow

o cean   the largest body of salt water on Earth

ore   rock that contains metals such as iron, copper, or gold

ox y gen   a gas that is released by plants and breathed in by animals

pen in su la   a piece of land that reaches out into the water from a larger body of land

phys i cal map   a map that shows the major landforms and bodies of water of a place

plain   a large area of mostly flat land

plate   a huge piece of Earth's crust that moves slowly across the mantle

pla teau   a large area of flat land that is higher than sea level

po lar   having to do with areas near the North or South poles

pol lut ed   to make unhealthy, as in *polluting the air and water*

port   a city where ships pick up and deliver cargo

pop u la tion   the number of people that live in a place

prai rie   treeless area with tall grass

pre cip i ta tion   wetness that falls from the sky as rain, snow, sleet, and hail; fog is also a form of precipitation

prime me rid i an the line on a globe that runs through the North and South poles and that divides Earth into the Eastern and Western hemispheres

raw ma te ri als the things from which a product is made, such as leather, rubber, and glue in shoes

re gion a group of places that have one or more things that are alike

re new a ble can be replaced

re source something we need or can use

riv er a large stream of fresh water

ro tate to spin or turn around

san i ta tion the act of preventing diseases by keeping things clean and safely getting rid of garbage and waste

sa van na a grassland found in warm climates that have both wet and dry seasons

sea a large body of salt water that is smaller than an ocean. Seas are partly surrounded by land.

sea le vel where the ocean meets the land

sea son a time of year, such as summer or winter

sed i ment the loose rocks, stones, sand, and soil carried away by streams and rivers

seis mo graph a sensitive machine that records movements within Earth's crust

smog dirty air made of fog, smoke, and chemicals

soil very fine bits of weathered rock mixed with living matter and the remains of plants and animals

steppe a grassland found in cool dry climates

swamp an area of soft, wet land

tem per ate not too hot and not too cold

tem per a ture how hot or cold something is

tor na do a violent, fast-moving column of air that extends downward from a cloud

trans port to carry

trop i cal having to do with the tropics, the warm moist regions around the equator

tro po sphere   the layer of the atmosphere closest to Earth

tun dra   a cold, treeless land where only tiny plants can grow in summer

val ley   a lowland between two mountains or mountain ranges

va por   very tiny droplets of water or other liquid floating in the air

veg e ta tion   the kinds of plants that grow in a place

vol can o   a break in Earth's surface through which melted rock flows

weath er   day-to-day changes in air temperature, winds, and precipitation

weath er ing   the softening and wearing away of rock